LED BY GOD

A Missionary's Story

MARC D. COOLS

TEACH Services, Inc.
P U B L I S H I N G
www.TEACHServices.com • (800) 367-1844

World rights reserved. This book or any portion thereof may not be copied or reproduced in any form or manner whatever, except as provided by law, without the written permission of the publisher, except by a reviewer who may quote brief passages in a review.

The author assumes full responsibility for the accuracy of all facts and quotations as cited in this book. The opinions expressed in this book are the author's personal views and interpretations, and do not necessarily reflect those of the publisher.

This book is provided with the understanding that the publisher is not engaged in giving spiritual, legal, medical, or other professional advice. If authoritative advice is needed, the reader should seek the counsel of a competent professional.

Copyright © 2023 Marc D. Cools
Copyright © 2023 TEACH Services, Inc.
ISBN-13: 978-1-4796-1538-4 (Paperback)
ISBN-13: 978-1-4796-1539-1 (ePub)
LOC: 2023902086

All Bible text references unless otherwise stated are taken from the King James Version of the Bible. Public domain.

Bible text references labeled (NIV) are taken from the Holy Bible, New International Version®, NIV® Copyright © 1973, 1978, 1984, 2011 by Biblica, Inc.® Used by permission. All rights reserved worldwide.

Published by

www.TEACHServices.com • (800) 367-1844

These memoirs are dedicated to my dear wife Adelheid who, from the very beginning, did not hesitate for a moment to follow me into an unknown world but dedicated herself to alleviating human suffering, both physical and spiritual. Secondly, we must not forget our two children, Heidi and Ben, who were born in this world that has become ours. Without neglecting the experience of the presence of God who was always at my side in the moments when everything went smoothly but also in the painful situations that seemed to me to have no way out.

"Weeping may endure for a night, but joy cometh in the morning" (Ps. 30:5).
Kehlen (Luxembourg) October 2018

Marc D. Cools

Table of Contents

Praise . . . . *vii*
Foreword . . . . *xi*
Introduction . . . . *xiii*

1. My Youth 15
2. Decisive Years 19
3. Newbold College 21
4. You Want to Talk About Coincidence? 23
5. Our Beginnings 27
6. On the Road 30
7. Please, Madam 35
8. Lost in the Night 41
9. The Lamp Goes Out 43
10. The Price of Water 45
11. The Churches that Burn 48
12. The Cursed Child 50
13. The Twin 52
14. A Day to Never Forget 55
15. Old Man David 60
16. The Locusts 63

17. Projects Come to Life 65
18. After 68
19. At Mount Cameroon 72
20. Douala 79
21. Oubenicam 85
22. Blocked on the Road 87
23. From One Mission Field to Another 95
24. Central African Republic (CAR) 101
25. On the Way to Ouadda 104
26. You're Going to Worship the Beast? 109
27. We Want to See… 111
28. What Does He Want from Me? 114
29. Our Father … You Know the Rest 117
30. Conferences in Bangui 124
31. Berberati 128
32. The Restaurant 134
33. Bangui and PK6 Nights 136
34. PK 22 138
35. The Enigma 140
36. The Return and After… 142

Praise

My son ..... gave me your book in which you tell about your missionary experience in Africa and Luxembourg. I read it with great pleasure. It brought back many memories. I would like to thank you....... For this living testimony.

—*Dr Richard Lehmann Prof. Emer.*
Collonges Adventist Seminary, France

For those who have not known the time of the heroic missions in Africa—which is my case—this testimony is fascinating. The time of the missions where a simple trip is an adventure, without insurance and without much comfort, where hours can become days or months, where the encounters are intense and sometimes blessed forever. A time when the missionary has to build everything on his own, when the relationship with God is experienced at every moment. A time when missionaries had neither mobile phones nor internet. A missionary remains a missionary forever. Reading his book will help you to discover this in turn.

—*Christian Sabot, Treasurer of the Belgo-Luxembourg,*
Belgian-Luxembourg Federation

I have read your book ...... I want to thank you for writing it. It is simply a book, and oh so rich in testimony and the blessings of our Lord. We need books like this.......

—*P. Charlier, assistant bank secretary /*
member of the Adventist church of Brussels Center

An interesting book written with the deep conviction that the Christian mission is still necessary today.

—*P.J., Director of ADRA Luxembourg*

Marc Cools reminds me of the hymn "Under the African sun, the pagan dies in the night," an aphorism that made me smile when I was wearing my first Sabbath pants in the church pews.

But in the meantime, my childish cynicism has turned into admiration, because Africa, so dynamic and fantastic, has conquered my missionary soul. It is therefore a pleasure to read this story written in a language that makes the charm of a polyglot author (using here and there a Dutch, English or Flemish turn of phrase). A book without length or embellishments, - thanks to the selective memory which, with the passing decades, allows one to concentrate on the essential.

More than his memoirs, the author reveals how God opens and closes doors at the right time and whose hand protects as long as He wishes to accomplish His purposes for us.

Led by God: the equivocation of the title is successful, Marc Cools having been as much "guided" as "piloted" by the Almighty. His testimony begins with a brief description of his call to ministry, followed by one miracle after another (we will not forget how the author was exempted from the Vietnam War).

Who is this author? A humble man concerned about the good of the "Work", and by his side, a woman whose consecration marked their children and countless African couples for eternity. We will note in passing the names of other missionaries; and then of course the Africans as we know them: heroes of the faith.

Pages that move you: the friendship of the Muslims with the Adventists, the baptism of a minister of finance; but also the lack of water and the torrential rains, the breakdowns and jams, or even getting lost in the bush where the missionary could well have died in the night. And to say that sweat and malaria are more the order of the day than electricity is not a cliché, but an everyday reality.

The new Africa is tarred and the airports repatriate you at the first emergency. Internet, cell phone, GPS: The new generation is well equipped. All the more reason to rekindle the spirit of sacrifice in us, because even if "the worries of the century and the seduction of riches" easily suffocate our zeal, this book upheaval testifies that there is still room for many harvesters.

All the more reason to see in this book a call that resounds in the tropical jungle (where corrugated iron still exists!) and in the concrete jungle of the metro poles of all continents: Let no one rest on laurels sown with the tears of the pioneers! Those who left their traces in the mud of the end of the world invite us to take over from the already beaten paths of the savannah to, in our turn, carry the torch to the confines of the darkness.

The story avoids sensationalism and heroism, and for those who are frightened by the bandits and other snakes on the lookout, it will be good to meditate on the magnificent biblical promises that embellish this book and put the weight of renunciation in the background to make the joy of being "led by God" sparkle.

Finally, let us note the intermittence between the accounts of Africa and Luxembourg - the third richest country in the world (GNP per capita) - reminding us that, in the meantime, the "heathen" is rather to be discerned in the fog of Europe than on a continent which, in its turn, could come to Macedonia to rescue us. Is it therefore a coincidence that the current pastor in charge of our churches in Luxembourg is Angolan?

—*Sylvain Romain, Researcher in Islamology*

Foreword

This is not a novel or a story about me as a central character. As you read the pages that follow, you would do well to open your eyes to appreciate how, over the course of a lifetime, God puts His hand and holds it on ordinary people. We must learn to open our eyes to discover the ways of God that are so often incomprehensible. Within each of us lies that unquenchable desire to succeed in life and, if possible, to do something great that will outlive us. But in all of this, we forget that Someone greater can often put his hand in our lives. Are we willing to find out? As soon as we come to this conclusion, it is no longer the "me" that counts, but we can give all the glory to the One who directed and protected. This is the purpose of the following lines. Nothing has been exaggerated.

"We will not hide them from their children, shewing to the generation to come the praises of the Lord, and his strength, and his wonderful works that he hath done" (Ps. 78:4).

In this account, apart from what God has done for me and my loved ones, I will also mention events that were passed on to me by responsible brothers who were visiting us. Meanwhile, many have already been put to rest, but I would like the miraculous acts of God in their regard to be preserved in the memory of our missions. If you find some inaccuracies in your reading, I apologize for this, as it is because of a defect in my memory. I have tried as best as possible to convey the events as they themselves have told them to us. If you, the reader, know more details or notice any errors on my part, I would be glad if you would let me know. It is unfortunate that our missionary reports are increasingly neglected in our churches. There is a divine power to be found there. God is not asleep these days. We are a worldwide church, and even the largest protestant church that is still protesting. Is there not a danger, however, that we limit ourselves to where we are and at the same time see how slowly the gospel is spreading in our regions? In the end, we get discouraged! Let us broaden our horizons, inquire beyond our borders and discover how the Lord is working all over the world to prepare a people for his return. "The field is the world" (Matt. 13:38).

I would like to emphasize again that this is neither a theological nor a philosophical work! It is simply an everyday fact. Days like the ones we live in every day.

Introduction

I have been thinking for a long time about writing down part of my life for the world that will outlive me. I am thinking especially of my children who may ask the question "but why and how did our father choose to be what he became?" I am not thinking here of my character but rather of being a pastor-missionary or missionary-pastor if you will.

It is a long story, it will take me a long time and it will have obstacles that I have always found immense because for a long time I have known that writing is not my forte. This is one of the reasons why I hesitated for so long to write these reflections on my life. I also encountered another difficulty. I have never kept a diary and many memories have been lost in the wind of the past years. However, it seems to me that the greatest moments still remain in my memory and I want to share them with you, dear children, dear readers. Looking back, I realize how God has kept me and guided me through often unexpected and difficult situations. All we have to do is open our eyes and be willing to see the miracles that God performs for us, miracles that seem, at first glance, to be the mundane things of everyday life, but in reality are much more than that. I have often been reminded of the song I learned in the MV (JA today): "Count God's blessings." There are indeed many. Again, just look at them!

I also want to pay tribute to my dear wife who has followed me without complaint wherever I have been called to serve our Master. She has not only followed me but also offered her services in a world of physical and spiritual suffering. We have always been a good team and we thank God for the many blessings we have witnessed.

I often refer in my Sabbath morning sermons or on other occasions to those great moments when I was able to meet the Lord more closely. Several people, including our children, have asked me to write these things down. I hesitated for a long time, but I'm starting now. I feel a bit of a push. I hope you will enjoy reading this testimony not just for joy or curiosity but to see how the Lord is working in everyone's life. "Taste and see that the Lord is good!" (Ps. 34:8).

1. My Youth

I am a child of the war years and grew up in an Adventist family. My parents didn't have it easy. Dad was fired from his job because of the Sabbath. After being drafted in 1939, he became a machinist in the Belgian army. One day, in order not to fall into enemy hands, near Ostend, he overheated his locomotive which, as a result, exploded. He then put on civilian clothes and walked more than 125 kilometers to reach his family in Antwerp. He then found work in a workshop. All this saved him from becoming a prisoner of war. My mother had a difficult birth in 1942 during the occupation. I was the one who arrived. After a few months, in the middle of winter, I caught a lung infection and the only doctor available in the area gave me little chance of survival.

A neighbor helped my mother save me from certain death with a remedy from ancient times by putting me in what was called a "hot mustard seed bath." Don't ask me what it is, but it does seem to have had a healing effect. My fever soon subsided, and I who was condemned was restored to life. How do I know all this? Well, my mom told me enough times so that I wouldn't forget what she considered to be a miracle. It was God who kept her child. I must also mention here that

My fever soon subsided, and I who was condemned was restored to life. How do I know all this? Well, my mom told me enough times so that I wouldn't forget what she considered to be a miracle.

our mother never stopped, since we were young, to regularly read us the Bible stories. She had a book for this purpose, in which she told the holy stories of the Old and New Testaments. As we grew up, we also received a little pocket money. It was never much, but enough to learn the value of money and our responsibility to God, as small as we were. If the amount was 1 franc, or even 5 francs on occasion, she had set up a cup for each of us in the cupboard for my brother and me to tithe into. We still had 10 or 25 centime coins with a hole in the middle. This learning from our childhood had a deep impact on us and played an important role later on, as you will understand a little later. We went to church every Sabbath and very often on foot with our grandfather. The distance was several miles. But we arrived on time for the start of Sabbath school.

Many years later, the time came to go to school. But another problem arose. Little Mark had a speech impediment, so much so that they planned to send me to a special school to learn to speak properly. In the end, everything was fine without a special school and years later, at the end of my first school year, I even got a prize from the city of Antwerp for my good speech and fluent reading.

My father had become a self-employed businessman, and he hoped that one day his two children would be able to join his company. My older brother was studying technology and I, three years younger, was studying accounting. We arrived here in the early 1960s. To understand what happened next, I have to go back to the early 1950s. "Man proposes and God disposes," as the saying goes.

Our church in Antwerp was led throughout these years by very enthusiastic pastors, full of love and convinced of the Adventist message, who did not leave aside their Christian and Adventist life when they were in the world. During those years, on June 21, 1958, to be precise, I was baptized in Antwerp by Pastor Deligne. I heard some sermons that I still remember today. One of them was by Pastor A. Deligne. One Sabbath morning during the service, he told an extraordinary missionary story that I have never forgotten. The story takes place in Algeria in the 1960s, at the time of the war of independence against France.

A 19 year old girl was kidnapped and after a 30 kilometers walk barefoot, the rebels decided to get rid of their victim and riddled her with bullets.[1] I still remember how Pastor Deligne presented this event in his sermon. Years have passed, Pastor A. Deligne went to his rest and I, now well advanced in age, have never forgotten this missionary story, although the details have left my memory. But recently I found a book written by Jean Kempf who spent his whole life in the mission fields, starting with Morocco and Algeria and then the CAR. In the pages of this book, *Il te montrera la voie*, I found the story firsthand with all the details. I strongly advise you to read this book by Jean Kempf. And for those who doubt, search the weekly *Paris Match* of that time. I found it myself in the May 16, 1959, edition. This extraordinary story also appeared in the *Revue Adventiste* of October 15, 1959.

Moreover, the Adventist Church had its congress each year in Brussels. This one took place in the Egmont & Hornes Convention Center. The 700 members of the Federation were present to listen to the sermons and missionary reports. Among the speakers were Dr. Nussbaum, a pioneer of religious freedom, and Jean Surrel, leader of our youth movement MV (Missionary Volunteer). Each of them spoke with conviction and from the heart.

One could feel that they were zealous for the gospel and its mission.

These brothers made me want to be a missionary! However, as time went by, I was destined for something else. My main goal was to go into Dad's business as an accountant. But events occurred that I had not counted on. Some problems in my training as an accountant, related to exams on the Sabbath, forced me to rethink my life path and finally ended up at the "Oud Zand-bergen" seminary in the Netherlands. There I successfully completed the training course for the pastorate. My original vision was revived. I thank my parents who always supported me in this

---

[1]"She was thrown to the ground by a violent shock, but she got up. The rebels, stunned, declared "She has baraka (luck), let's not kill her"... The bandits hung Marie-José's blouse in their camp and nearly two hundred of them paraded in front of this garment to contemplate this extraordinary thing." *: Jean & Sigrid Kempf: *Il te montrera la voie*, p. 212.

crucial decision of my life. One day when I was visiting home, we had to go see Grandma. A former coffee shop owner, she was disappointed in me and couldn't understand how my parents could so easily let me enter a branch of life that she herself had no concept of and considered to be nothing. My father's response to her: "Mom, God gave me two sons: one for me, the other for God. So be it!" This remark, so quick and convincing, has followed me to this day.

> *"Mom, God gave me two sons: one for me, the other for God. So be it!"*

2. Decisive Years

After I left business school and before I went to seminary, Dad found me a job in Germany with a friend who had a mattress factory near Frankfurt. I could go to work for him to earn some money to pay for my seminary studies. It was a whole new experience for me. Soon I would be 18 years old and it was the first time I really left my father's house and it was for Germany. In 1960, the war had only been over for fifteen years and the country was booming, so there was plenty of work. The train trip was quite an adventure. The trains were still pulled by a steam locomotive and at the entrance to the station in Aachen, there were gates everywhere to guide passengers to the exits. Soon the train continued on its way to Frankfurt on the Main. Dad's friend had sent me some postage stamps that once I arrived in Frankfurt, I had to exchange at the post office to get DMs so that I would have money to call him when I arrived, which I did without delay. After my phone call, he came to pick me up and half an hour later I was on my way to Neu-Isenburg, the place of my future residence. For the first time in my life I was going to earn money. I had a good salary and I was already looking forward to a good life. To better understand one of my actions as a young man, I have to go back a few years. On special occasions, my mother would surprise us with a bottle of apple juice, which she called "Apfelwein" ("apple wine"). But one bottle was not much for a family of four, so we received a little bit each in a special glass for the occasion. It was just enough to taste it and make us want more! Now, years later, having become independent and having some money in my pocket, one evening after work my steps took me to a store to buy a bottle of

"Apfelwein", this time all for myself. But I was astonished to discover that the taste was not the same and I soon discovered that I had not bought Mom's good product but real apple wine, "cider", at I don't know how many degrees. I remember drinking two glasses and then sleeping well. From that day on, I never bought "Apfelwein" again but only real apple juice, the one my mother used to serve us!

Dad's friend was an avid member of the Adventist Church and of course I accompanied his family to church every Sabbath. How fortunate! The first Sabbath I attended service, I met a young blonde girl who, after five years, became my dear wife! She was also working nearby waiting to enter nursing school a few months later. When the time was up, she went to Düsseldorf to start her nursing studies and I, after a detour to Antwerp, went to the Netherlands to start my theology studies. The only means of communication we had at that time were letters sent by post (and the mail was often slow), occasionally a phone call (very rare) or possibly a short surprise visit. After three years, I moved away again to study at Newbold College in England. My dear Adelheid was still in Düsseldorf. But after finishing the seminary in the Netherlands and before going to Newbold, Reinder, Dieter, and I decided to go to Sweden to peddle and make some money to pay for our studies. There we were able to work well and our school future seemed secure. After three months of intense door-to-door selling of our books, we all went home and a few weeks later we found ourselves in England.

3. Newbold College

When I finished my studies at the seminary of "Oud Zandbergen" in the Netherlands, I went to England to Newbold College. Regularly, once a week, we could join a group to go colporteuring. This was an opportunity to earn part of the study costs or to make some pocket money from time to time. I sometimes accompanied this group to make some pocket money. The college car would take us to the designated location and in the evening we would be picked up at a specific spot for the return and the count. I was never a great colporteur and never liked it, although I had months of experience in Sweden behind me. But necessity dictates! That day was unforgettable for me. The sale was not extraordinary, but I can't forget the following.

It was a row of houses with a small garden in front of the entrance as one often finds. I rang the bell and, as usual, we waited for the surprise of who we would meet. An old lady opens to me. She listens to me kindly and at the end of my speech, she points out to me that her daughter is absent and she cannot help me. Could I come back another time? Having apologized to her for having disturbed her and thanked her for her kindness, full of courage, I continue towards the next door. Again a long wait. Just as I want to leave, the door opens, and who do I see? Again an old lady like the previous one. My mind works very fast and to avoid making the same speech to hear the same answer as the previous one, I ask her if her daughter is at home. She looks at me with mean eyes and says to me very meanly: "My daughter has been married for a long time and you have nothing to do with her" and the door closes with a loud bang. I found myself as if nailed to the floor. I quickly realized my stupidity, but as I walked away, I couldn't help but burst out laughing.

The student I was rooming with at Newbold was from the United States. His name was James Thurmon and we soon became good friends. It was James who convinced me to go to the U.S. to finish college at Southern, in Tennessee. But before I could realize this plan, which had become a dream, I had to get some things in order. Would my fiancée, who was studying in Germany at that time, agree to start our life together in an unknown country far from her homeland? She did not object. We had planned to get married before we left. The only problem was that after the wedding she had to return to Düsseldorf for three months to take her final exams and I had to leave immediately so that I wouldn't miss the start of classes at SMC. (I must not forget to mention the support I received from my parents for my studies in Newbold and to move to the USA). After three months of separation, I received a telegram telling me that she had passed her exams and she arrived a few days later.

4. You Want to Talk About Coincidence?

Adelheid immediately found a job in a hospital not far from the college. With her German diploma, she was soon recognized as a registered nurse (RN). Thanks to her, I was able to finish my studies at Southern without financial problems. No, that's not quite true. I have to tell you about the miracle we experienced together!

Student life is not always without financial problems. To be honest, the income at the end of the month barely covered our household expenses without doing anything "extra." At the end of the month, our first action was to set aside the "tithes" for the Lord. To keep them well set aside, we decided to put the money belonging to God in an empty jar (a bit like I had learned from my mother as a child). We could then put them in a tithe envelope the next Sabbath. However, one day our pockets were empty, but not only our pockets but also the cupboards and the fridge. What to do? We looked at our jar of God's money and wondered if we could not borrow for once from the One to whom everything belongs. After praying, we decided not to borrow anything from Him, asking Him to provide for our needs in His way. My wife left in the morning as she did every day for Cleveland, Tennessee, where she worked and I left during the day. When I got home, I wondered how God was going to provide for us. I didn't find a miracle when I got home. With a great hollowness in my stomach and to escape any temptation, I went to the library. When Adelheid came home in the evening, I went up to the apartment to wait for her arrival.

A little later, I saw her getting out of the car with a big smile. Soon I understood the reason for her good mood. A patient at the hospital had given her $20—he had appreciated her care so much that he had given her the money! Just enough for us to make ends meet. Thank you, Lord! We have never forgotten that moment. Since then, we have never failed to trust the One who says: "The world is mine and all that is in it" (Ps. 50:12). This was one of the first miracles we experienced early in our married life!

To cover all the expenses of the month, I also had several kinds of jobs that occupied much of my time outside of school. One of them was in a "French Lab" to teach proper pronunciation to those studying French, another was a night job in the McKee Baking Company. But the latter also had its price. I sometimes fell asleep in class. Then the loud voice of the teacher coming from the front of the class would quickly wake me up: "Marc Denis!" But how else could we do it? We had to live!

Yet toward the end of the year, an unexpected obstacle surfaced. During those years, the United States was in the middle of a war in Vietnam. With 500,000 troops engaged in that far-off land, "Uncle Sam" needed

Our House in Collegedale, TN, USA

4. You Want to Talk About Coincidence?   25

recruits, and so one day I received an order from the Army to "report to a location in Tennessee to be drafted into the army." At that moment, I deeply regretted coming to the United States on an immigrant visa. Now I had no way to avoid the call to arms. No Belgian embassy in the country could help me. Having chosen the American advantages, I now also had duties. What to do and how? Nobody could help me! Except for my wife who confided in me that she had been pregnant for a month. To be honest, I wasn't expecting it, but it was my salvation. Soon enough, a medical certificate was enough for me to receive the following note from the army: "as an expectant father you are exempt from military service." Coincidence? Talk about a happy accident! The school year went on without further incident. After graduation, I wanted to leave the country of a thousand possibilities as soon as possible. I must intervene here to express my deep gratitude to God for saving me from the carnage in Vietnam. I recently saw a documentary film about this horrible war. It was then that I really realized what the Lord had saved me from. My life was probably going to take a whole new turn. I am so thankful for the way God has taken over my life. I am sure that He saved me and that He had other plans for me.

Instead of landing in Asia, I now had several job offers in a few Unions in the United States but I preferred to leave. To that end, I wrote to the president of my home federation, Georges Vandenvelde, but to my amazement, I never received a reply. After a month of waiting, I asked the General Conference if they needed a missionary couple. A week later, I received a letter from Brother Pierson who was the GC president at that time, stating that my home division was looking for a missionary in Cameroon. In the Middle East, specifically in Cairo, it also needed men. Two weeks later, the final decision was made: Cameroon.

After various medical visits, two months later, we received the plane tickets to New York and for the trip by boat to Europe. A visit to my home division was necessary for more precise information. My first visit to Belgium was to the conference offices. To my great surprise, no one here knew about the situation. But it was also here that a mystery was revealed to me. My letter of application to the conference had never arrived in

Brussels. Did God have other plans for us? Second surprise: no one knew about our departure for Cameroon. Contact was immediately made with the division offices. Fortunately, they were well and truly informed of our imminent departure. However, we had to wait another month. This period was considered as a kind of departure leave to visit our respective families. Finally, we received our tickets! Fortunately, I realized that we had made a mistake in our destination. We were supposed to leave by boat from Marseille to Douala, the economic capital of Cameroon, but the tickets indicated Durban, South Africa as the final port.

Finally, everything was put in order. A week later, we left Antwerp by train for Paris-Marseille where a brother picked us up at the station and took us to a hotel for one night. But soon, one night became seven! The reason: the strike at the port of Marseille. There is nothing fun about being stranded in a city you don't know, knowing just a few basics of the local language. My knowledge of the French language was limited to what I had learned while attending school in Antwerp. In addition, one evening we were invited to the home of the pastor of the church in Marseille and he asked me to plan the preaching for the next Sabbath. I tried to get out of it, but to him my French seemed sufficient and besides, I was a missionary on my way to Africa, I surely had something to tell. I assure you that I was very happy when Sabbath morning was over, but at the same time I was amazed at what I had still retained from my language courses in Antwerp. Or had God loosened my tongue?

A few days later, the brother in charge (whose name I have forgotten) informed us of a change of travel and at the same time of the release of our hotel room. Our boat tickets were changed into plane tickets. In a few days we were to leave for Douala. But there was still a "but"! Since my wife was in her seventh month of pregnancy, she needed a medical certificate to travel by plane. Fortunately, this visit did not reveal anything abnormal and a few days later we were finally on our way to Douala, Yaoundé, Nanga Eboko.

5. Our Beginnings

The flight from Marseille to Douala went smoothly. For the one from Douala to Yaoundé, it was something else! Crammed into an old DC6, it was much less comfortable and gave us a real taste of what awaited us on African soil. In Yaoundé we were met by Brother H. Walder who was the treasurer of the union. After passing through customs, where we were searched from top to bottom, and fortunately assisted by the union representative, we set off through Yaoundé to the Walder house where we spent our first night under the African sky. The next day we were shown around the union offices and the Adventist printing house. That same day, Brother Adolphe Kinder arrived and the next day he drove us to Nanga Eboko, after 160 kilometers of dirt track and savanna! The villages along the road gave us a first impression of the country where we had landed. Houses built of earth, with a roof of palm leaves or bananas. A way of life where it seems that everyone lives in the street. Children playing with old bicycle rims or homemade toys. And suddenly, a herd of cows on the road in the opposite direction to the capital, which will constitute the daily meat consumption of the local population. During this trip, we were shaken endlessly because of the state of the road. It was not tarred but covered with simple laterite which raised huge clouds of dust, behind or in front of us, depending on the direction of the traffic. Let's not forget that we were on one of the main roads of the country connecting the south and the north. What a world we had arrived in! Once we arrived at our destination, Adolphe Kinder, president of the Nanga Eboko mission, explained our task within the mission. In fact, up to that point, no one had let us know what work we were being sent to do in Cameroon. Communication was still old-fashioned, with letters that often took weeks to reach their destination. Brother Kinder finally enlightened us. His wife, who was in charge of the mission dispensary, had to return to France for health reasons and her husband had to follow her a month later. We began to understand what it was all about. Going from a state-of-the-art hospital in the United States to a clinic in the African bush, what a difference for Adelheid! For me, fresh out of college and now parachuted in as a mission president in an Africa I didn't know, you can imagine! And all this without forgetting that my wife Adelheid was seven months pregnant! Having been shaken up on the way to Nanga, wouldn't the baby arrive before the due date? In any case, on the day of the birth, we would have to make our way back to Yaoundé. Brother Kinder was there for a month to introduce me to the daily work, but my wife had to start the next day at the clinic, which was full of patients. A good nurse's aide assisted her. We have forgotten his name.

After a few days of working in the paperwork of the mission office, I started learning how to visit and travel in the bush. For this, I needed a lot of equipment. It was to be a sort of camping, spending days and nights in the bush villages but without the comfort of European campsites! No electricity, no drinking water, no toilets and a mosquito net was absolutely necessary to avoid being eaten by mosquitoes. After these few weeks during which Brother Kinder made me know the extent of the mission, here he is leaving! Now we had to manage on our own, counting on God's grace. A few more details: at the mission station in Nanga there was also the Adventist college. Several other teaching brothers also lived on the mission territory or, if you prefer, the mission was on the college campus.

From this point of view, we were not alone. However, as far as work was concerned, everything was very separated. This reassured me because, being absent most of the time from Friday to Sunday or Monday, I knew that my wife wasn't alone and that there would be help for her at her time of delivery.

Brother Kinder brought me precious help, not only for the office work but also for the tours in the bush. He became my right hand during the months at Nanga: Brother Engozo Daniel; I must also mention Thomas Bendele.

6. On the Road

Let's begin with Thomas, a tireless pastor, always on the road from morning to night. He had an old moped. Jesus was his friend whom he had to go and preach and serve. He was a tireless man of the field. No journey with his means of travel was too much for him. No job was impossible for him and he was always available with a big smile. He was the one who would visit the most distant churches in time for baptisms and Communion. I learned a lot from him, starting with his love for the people and the service of the ministry as well as in the field of relations with Africans. One day, after a week's absence, he came to me to tell me about a problem he had encountered in some churches. It was during a tour in the bush where he had gone to serve communion. At one point, he realized that he did not have enough grape juice. It is important to know that we received concentrated grape juice in small cans that we had to mix with water on the spot. The union obtained these cans in Europe and sent them to the different missions. When a pastor needed it, he would come to the office to get it according to the number of churches to be served. I don't remember if the number of cans was insufficient at that time or if he didn't take enough. In any case, he ran out of juice along the way. The mission being far away, at a distance of several days by moped, it was unthinkable for him to return to renew his stock. He wondered what to do. The members were waiting for him impatiently. He then made an arrangement with Jesus. There are drinks in these villages, not only beer (available everywhere) but also lemonade. Our good brother Thomas got a pomegranate lemonade (which is also red) in one of these bush villages

6. On the Road

Faced with an insurmountable obstacle

and used it as a symbol of Christ's blood. What would I have done in his place? If I remember correctly, I took it with a sense of humor, because you have to be able to manage!

Brother Engozo was my faithful travel companion. He knew every passable and impassable route. One day, when I left in a car, an old Taunus, far from home, the road seemed really impeccable. However, he had warned me that there was a bridge ahead which, according to his description, could cause difficulties. Wouldn't it be better to take a longer but safer route? I had probably not understood correctly.

I must remind you that my French was still in the learning stage and that of Engozo was better but Africanized and not always easily understandable for me. After kilometers and kilometers, we arrived at the famous bridge. A stream had dug its way through the road and a kind of bridge had been made by simply throwing down two big beams. After inspecting them and the width and depth they covered, we decided not to take any chances, although we were tempted to try. Later, we thanked the

Lord that we had not taken that risk. We would never have arrived at our destination but probably in the swamp, 3 meters below.

Another trip took place in "no man's land." By this I mean the savannah some 150 kilometers from the mission. It is worth remembering that during this period, there were no mobile phones–which means that when we were lost, we were really lost! Suddenly a big plume of smoke came out of the engine. I immediately turned off the ignition. I opened the hood and, soon after, the fire that had started stopped. It should be said that I know nothing about mechanics. After opening the hood, we found nothing special. We were now stuck on a track in the middle of the savannah, without knowing what to do. The only thing my brother Engozo could tell me was that here, on a "track of tracks", cars rarely, if ever, passed. One could only hope that they would notice our absence from the mission and start looking for us. What to do in such a situation? It was simple, we started to pray. Prayer was part of our life. In the morning, before our trips, on the road, on the way back, we asked God to accompany us. After asking heaven to help us, we began to wait, recounting episodes we had experienced together. An hour later, we heard the sound of a heavy truck. It was not a "fata morgana" (a mirage). No, a few moments later, a big truck was turning back. In such a situation, you can be sure of being rescued. It would have to encroach on the savannah in order to pass our car that was blocking the way, and without asking any further questions, the driver took us in his cab and drove us to the mission. A certain Brother Legal, attached to the Adventist college for general maintenance and to the mission, accompanied me the next day to pick up and repair the car. He had a "deux chevaux" at his disposal. I must admit that with such a vehicle, one can go everywhere. When we arrived at the place where we had left my car, he quickly found the problem. I was happy to be back. It was late but I was safe. During the evening prayer, my wife and I did not forget to thank the Lord for his help at the right time.

The next episode that I will never forget is the trip to the country of the "Maka." Brother Engozo had advised me to go there during a long weekend. It was not too far away and the church members were waiting for me impatiently. Since everything was in short supply in these places, the pastors were always eager to bring all kinds of goods, including pants and shirts. Since this was a region with many churches and many workers, my Taunus was loaded to the max. After about 100 kilometers, I realized that something was not right. It seemed to me that the car was starting to sag. After stopping to check, I saw that both rear suspensions were broken and that the spring leaves were resting on the body. What to do? Go back to the mission or keep going in the hope that it would hold up on the bush track? Engozo encouraged me by telling me that we were almost there! Relying on his Word and the grace of God, we decided to continue. After an hour, I asked, "Is it much farther?" "No, no, it's just after the next turn, a little farther." Driving slowly because of the broken suspension, I saw the time passing and it seemed to me that the journey was endless. However, Engozo continued to encourage me with the same words: "No, it's not far, we are almost there." In a short time, the sun was going to set and to be honest, I started to worry: would we arrive? Would the suspension hold until the end of the trip? When it got dark in the forest, Engozo showed signs of worry. "Why are you nervous?" I asked him. Touching my arm and taking it between his fingers, he replied, "That's the best part! You, pastor, don't have to worry because you are white and white people are counted but we black people are not. One more or less, nobody will notice." When the sun had completely disappeared, we arrived at the village where the entire community was eagerly waiting for us. The church filled up quickly. After words of thanks to our Lord and prayers from the congregation, we took our places of honor near a bonfire and the members presented biblical scenes with mimes and various songs. It was midnight when I was able to retire to my hut for a well-deserved rest. I think that Engozo was even happier to retire

Don't ask me how the suspension on the car was able to hold up during that long bush tour, but I am sure that the Lord was there involved for something.

to his bed after a day that was much more stressful for him than for me. The next day, at the morning worship, the car had been quickly relieved of its contents and I noticed with relief that the Taunus had lifted a little. We continued our tour without any other notable problems. Don't ask me how the suspension on the car was able to hold up during that long bush tour, but I am sure that the Lord was there involved for something.

"In you, LORD my God, I put my trust" (Ps. 25:1, NIV).

7. Please, Madam

The day arrived when my wife was to give birth. We started the journey to Yaoundé. The bumps on the road brought the delivery forward. That same night, Adelheid was taken to the hospital for delivery. But in the end, our daughter who was to be born was unexpectedly delayed and the doctor on duty decided to intervene by cesarean section. The good sister nurse who was present probably realized the seriousness of the situation and constantly gave encouragement by making signs to the sky by which she probably wanted to make it clear that in case of a catastrophic turn of events, heaven would receive their souls well. In the end, the operation went well. However, there was a shortage of nursing staff to transport my dear wife to her room. Fortunately, I remained present during the complicated delivery because the honor fell to me to transport my wife to her room, with the help of someone passing by at the right time in the right place. But the main thing is that we became the proud parents of a beautiful blonde girl whom we named Heidi. However, it doesn't end there. Two days later, my wife got sick with staphylococcus and I got dengue fever, also called bush fever, which causes terrible headaches. The missionaries in Yaoundé took good care of us. After two weeks, Adelheid was able to leave the hospital and I also recovered. The next day we set out for Nanga Eboko. Adelheid didn't have much extra time to rest because there were many sick people waiting at the clinic. Soon a friendship and good understanding developed between the hospital in Nanga and its doctor on the one hand, and the dispensary and Adelheid on the other, both institutions being used to receiving a constant flow of patients. One day, the doctor from the hospital came to visit us with a special request. At the hospital, one of his good and faithful nurses had lost his wife during her 8th delivery. The poor man was completely lost and did not know what to do with his large family and especially his newborn baby. "Please, Madam, can't you take care of this little jewel? At least until the child has grown up a bit?" We didn't have to think long and placed a little blonde baby with a little African baby in the same crib. Never has a family grown so fast, I think!

We also looked after a leper station. Leprosy is a terrible disease that eats away at the extremities of the human body. Fortunately, today there are medicines that can prevent the disease from continuing to eat away at the limbs and even cure people. Every month, they came to the clinic to get their tablets. These medicines were made available to them free of charge by the Cameroonian state. But unfortunately, leprosy was often noticed late or care was neglected. The tablets could stop the disease, but the fingers and toes were already eaten away. A village was planned for these lepers. I have forgotten the name of the village, but these people had settled there with their families. They were working their fields in rather difficult circumstances and were regularly supplied with rice and other foodstuffs. We were careful not to forget the day of the "Raoul Follereau" foundation. Apart from this important day for them, I went there quite often. We also had a church there that was well attended.

Here is how to attach the machete to work in the field

Every time I went there, I thought about the times when Jesus healed many: once "one" (Mark 1), another time "ten" (Luke 17). We look forward to the time when Jesus will return and wipe out the terrible disease of sin once and for all. "...There will be no more mourning or crying or pain" (Rev. 21:4).

7. Please, Madam

A few months later, the Augsburger family, then working in Dogba, and a missionary who was in the north near Maroua, were moving to Bafang. We were asked to move to the north of the country. The need was twofold: a pastor and a nurse who could take care of a large dispensary where many deliveries had to be handled. Our move took place in November. After only eight months in Nanga, we left for Dogba, a thousand kilometers further in the North of the country. In an old DC6, well shaken in the air, we arrived in Maroua where we were welcomed by Brother René Augsburger. After a journey of about 30 kilometers, once again shaken on the northern tracks, we arrived at the mission station of Dogba. It was founded by Brother Ruben Bergström in the 1930s. Apart from the new house built in the 1950s, the house of the first missionary R. Bergström was still intact and inhabited by an African family. When Bergström left, he was replaced by Albert Bodenmann who moved to Ndjamena (then called Fort Lamy) in early 1960. It was he who had learned (like Brother Bergström) the Foulani language to have more direct access to the population. Bodenmann is also the pioneer of Adventist work in Chad. We went together to see the land in Béré where the dispensary that became the Adventist hospital of Chad was later built. This was 1968.

The terrible disease.
People without fingers or toes

Let us return to our new assignment. Soon the Augsburgs were gone and we were alone again. There were no other missionary couples there except at the Adventist hospital in Koza, 100 kilometers away.

Occasionally, we were visited by the doctor of this hospital for serious and difficult cases. The doctor on duty in Koza at that time was Dr. Koliah Steveny. My wife quickly learned the Foulani language and thus had an easy rapport with the Muslim women of the village. When I look back now fifty years, I realize that our missionary work really began here. We were alone and depended on the grace of God. We had a very good relationship with the villagers on the other side of the marigot. Adelheid was much appreciated for her good and faithful service to the native population who came from near and far. I will come back to this later. I personally had a very good relationship with Bakari, the chief of the Muslim part of the village. There were times when I asked him for advice, and he did the same for me, about how things should work. Let me give you an example: one day, in the village, a man complained against someone from the mission (I don't remember the details). Bakari didn't know what to do. He came to me and asked me what I thought and what to do.

We had to return our adopted baby from Nanga before we left for Dogba. This left a certain void in the family. In February, we were expecting our second baby. The doctor at the hospital in Maroua advised us to go to Yaoundé for the delivery, because of the previous cesarean section. Two months before the big moment, Adelheid had to fly to Yaoundé with little Heidi. Those were the most difficult two months for me, two months all alone at the Dogba station. But God is good, I learned patience and trust. I was busy teaching at the school we had created to train young pastors. At the station there were also two elementary school classes. I got along very well with the two school teachers, Amos and Houli, and they were real friends. Our nurse's aide at the clinic, Daimon, had to manage during my wife's absence. After the happy event, Adelheid resumed her place in our little family and in the clinic. Everyone was happy to see her again, especially the patients.

One day I was invited by an evangelist worker to come and meet the people he had prepared for baptism and at the same time to see the place where it would take place. I couldn't get there in a Land Rover because the banks of the river (which was dry at that time of year) were too high and on the other side there wasn't even a track to drive on. We (a young devotee named Sanda accompanied me) borrowed bicycles and set off.

7. Please, Madam

After a journey of several hours in the hot sun, we reached a village at the foot of the mountains. The place was beautiful.

After the examination of the candidates, we went to the place chosen for the baptisms. I wondered where we could find water here, in this place lost in the savannah, and in the middle of the dry season. After climbing up a narrow and rocky path, we arrived at a beautiful water basin. Words fail me to describe it. On one side, the water was falling into the basin and the surplus was coming out on the other side. I had never seen such a beauty of nature, in such a dry place.

The baptistry made by God

A baptistery perfectly made by the hands of God. After visiting this beautiful place and returning to the village, we had another meeting with the members and candidates. When we finished our visit, it was time to go back. The sun was starting to set and sunset is fast in the tropics. But on the way back came what I didn't expect. On the trail, full of rocks and thorns, not one but both tires of my bike broke. We had no choice but to walk back, bikes in hand. The worst part of the situation was that I had not worn proper shoes but simple beach shoes, flip flops, indeed good for the beach but surely unsuitable for the bush. The worst was yet to come. At one point, we heard amazing noises but we could hardly see anything, so much darkness had taken over the sky! My companion Sanda (with the same shoes as me) acted as if he hadn't heard anything and faithfully followed me as if nothing was wrong. When the sound got louder, I asked him: where could this unsettling noise be coming from? Loudly and almost with a smile, as I understood him and imagined his manner of speaking, he replied: "Oh! That's nothing, Pastor, it's just the slithering sound of the big snake following us!" Not believing what he said, I asked him to repeat himself, as if I hadn't understood well. He repeated what he had just told me, adding quickly: "But don't worry, Pastor, God is big!" Courageously, he continued on the way and my heart had practically jumped into my throat. To be frank, I was happy to arrive an hour later safe and sound at the mission. Since that night, the verse from Job 36:26 "How great is God–beyond our understanding!" has never left my mind. This young brother taught me, by reciting the first part of this verse, a lesson that I could never forget. His great faith and his knowledge of the scriptures became an example for me to imitate to this day. Thank you, Lord, for the example of Sanda, the young man who taught me a profound lesson! Years later, Sanda became a pastor!

8. Lost in the Night

One evening (it was already dark because the sun sets early in Africa), we heard a man's voice calling from the terrace of the house: "madam, madam....," accompanied by the barking of the dog. When we met him on the doorstep, he explained that his wife had been in labor pains for quite some time. "Please, can't you come help us?" Since we had two small children at home and the location seemed quite remote, we decided that I alone would go and get the woman and my wife would stay with our two little ones waiting for our return. I set off in the Land Rover, accompanied by the husband who had to show me the way, which is not so easy in the dark. We were in the middle of the rainy season, corn, cotton and other crops were growing. Let us add that at this time of the year, the traditional roads are very often flooded, the bridges are cut, and we had to look for unusual passages. My dear guide of that night constantly indicated to me: "here, there, straight ahead" etc. In the days before GPS or cell phones, I had no choice but to follow my companion's directions with the car's headlights as the only vision illuminating a black hole in the void in front of me. I started to wonder: would we get there? Did the man still know where he was? Then suddenly, after multiple "left...right...etc.," the man who was to become a father became a bit nervous (this is already unusual for an African) and finally, he broke down and admitted that he was lost and this in the middle of a cotton field. He asked me to stop so he could reorient himself. Personally, I had no idea where we could be. I just hoped he could find his way. In front, behind, to the left, to the right, I could only see the darkness and above, the sky sparkling with stars. What to do?

After a moment of reflection, my companion got out of the car and said, "please follow me, I'm running ahead in the light of your headlights, I know we're not far." Here we go again. To my amazement, he was running (really running, in the full sense of the word) with the Land Rover's headlights now pointed at him. As I followed him, a story from the Bible came to mind: Elijah running ahead of Ahab's chariot in a torrential downpour to show him the way (1 Kings 18:46). But this time it wasn't rain but darkness, and I was the one who needed someone to run ahead to show the way and so I felt like Ahab. When we arrived at the village, we loaded the poor lady into the car, hoping that we would arrive in time for the delivery. The return trip, the route now known, went without too much difficulty. When we arrived at the clinic, my wife was faced with a complicated delivery. That same night, I drove the lady another 30 kilometers farther to the hospital in Maroua.

9. The Lamp Goes Out

In spite of our daily occupations, Adelheid at the dispensary and I with the daily business of the mission, our children were walking with their "boys" in the village belonging to the mission at the other end of the station. This is where my faithful service companions Sanda and Togloko lived. Our daughter Heidi regularly went to this predominantly Adventist village to play with the other village children. To get there, we had to cross a hundred meters of no-man's land. On one side of the road that led to the village was the first house built by Brother Bergström in the 1930s, and on another side was a kind of silo where the villagers carried their harvest of millet to be stored in times of crisis. For the rest of the distance from our house to the mentioned village, there was nothing but a few bushes and palm trees. Once the sun went down, we had to make the journey with a flashlight or a storm lamp. Also, during the night, it was not advisable to move around because of the danger of hyenas or other animals that roamed around during the dark hours. I will give you some examples.

At one point, Brother Bergström encountered one of these animals. As he left his house in the evening, he saw two eyes looking at him in the distance. He immediately thought: "a panther." As quickly as he had gone out, he went back in to get his rifle. On his way out, he quickly aimed at the glowing eyes in the dark and fired. He realized a little later that he had shot his own dog. The animal did not survive. To show the danger of the night, here is my own experience. We had a chicken coop behind the house. We had a few fresh eggs every day. But one day, I started to notice that a chicken was regularly missing in the morning. The next day, another one was missing. I was now paying attention during the night. That's right! Around midnight, we heard a screech in the chicken coop and a hen was missing again in the morning. When I consulted my African brothers, for them it could only be a hyena. I went to the chief of the Muslim village, my friend Bakari, on the other side of the marigot, to ask him for help by lending me his rifle, which he did without further complication, giving me not only his rifle but also plenty of cartridges. The next night, when I stood guard with the rifle in my hands, the animal came back. That was the only time in my life I ever used a gun. Bad shooter that I am, I saved my chickens but missed the hyena. One night, our dog was also attacked by one of these wild beasts. He too paid with his life. All this is to remind us that it was not safe to travel around our house at night.

One day, after the evening meal, with the sun already down, my wife and I were still at the table, talking about the day's events. Nothing more than routine business, but enough to give us something to talk about. Suddenly, we heard a child crying and screaming in the distance. What was going on? It couldn't have been our latest child; he was sleeping peacefully in his crib. But Heidi, where was she? We called her, but there was no answer. As we listened a little more carefully, we realized that the crying was coming from far away and that it was our daughter's voice. I immediately grabbed my flashlight and, guided by the screams, ran into the darkness. And what did I see? In the middle of nothing, I found our daughter with a storm lamp that had stopped providing light in the dark and dangerous night! I assure you that she was very happy to find her daddy and he was happy to find his daughter. She never went out at night again with a lamp that seemed to give the assurance of seeing clearly. We had no reason to be angry because we were too happy to find our treasure safe and sound in our arms.

Isn't there a parable where Jesus tells the story of ten girls who went with their lamps to meet the bridegroom? But five of their lamps went out (Matt. 25) and in Luke 11:35, Jesus says: "Take heed therefore that the light that is in thee be not darkness."

10. The Price of Water

One day I had to go to Fort Lamy, today N'Djamena. A meeting was scheduled with Brother Bodenmann to go and see a piece of land for the establishment of a dispensary, which as now become the hospital of Bere. The Union had decided to set up a clinic there in addition to the mission that Bodenmann had begun in the capital to launch medical work in Chad. The place chosen was Béré. I was invited by our brother Bodenmann to accompany him to see the land that the government had offered us. While today there is a paved road between Maroua and N'Djamena, in those days it was a little-used track through the steppes of northern Cameroon and a ferry was used to cross the river Chari to reach the capital of Chad. The trail was difficult to travel during the rainy season and very dusty during the dry season in temperatures that could easily reach 35°C. The distance between these two cities was more or less 270 kilometers and it took a whole day to cover the journey. I left early in the morning to enjoy the coolness of the day. Gadabak, my friend who faithfully accompanied me during my travels everywhere, accompanied me as usual that day. The trips in these regions are always full of unexpected events, it is indeed inadvisable to travel alone, especially for such distances. When I reached the halfway point, the sun started to shine more and more. I noticed something strange while driving the Land Rover. The car started to lose power. The harder I pressed the gas pedal, the more difficult it was for the car to move forward and it seemed to brake. What was going on? A little later, smoke came out of the engine and everything stopped. I studied Greek and Hebrew, but I seemed to have missed taking a car mechanics course because I was now stuck in the middle of the bush/savannah with the car's engine stuck and smoking. After examining the situation, I realized that the radiator water inlet hose had failed and the engine coolant was missing. This was the reason why the engine had overheated and stalled.

I didn't want to use the drinking water I had on hand to fill the radiator because putting cold water in a radiator and circulating it through an overheated engine can cause it to burst. If that happened, I would have no car and no water to survive. So I turned myself to Gadabak (the courier) with the intention of asking him to go and get water somewhere. Maybe he would find a village here or there where we could be helped? It seems to me that he wasn't too keen on the idea of going in search of water. However, Gadabak left and I watched him disappear over the horizon, hoping that he would succeed. In my heart I prayed, "Lord, help us." When Gadabak disappeared on the horizon, I was all alone and I had nothing to do but wait. In such a situation, every minute seemed like an eternity. Fortunately, a bird from here and there in the bushes around me regularly came to keep me company and could be heard with a beautiful whistle.

I was waiting. Gadabak had already been gone for an hour to get water. Finally, I saw him reappear at the end of the path he had taken. As he approached, I noticed that he had something in his hand. Had he managed to find water to refill the radiator? Yes, he had water, but a small calabash containing no more than a liter.

Is that all?

"Yes sir, in the village I found, the people told me that they could not give me more because there is a lack of water in their house (by them)."

Which is understandable, I thought.

Now we just had to wait together, hoping that someone would come by. Heaven knows our situation. Around three o'clock in the afternoon, a cloud formed on the horizon. A car approached, help in sight? It could only pass by as it entered the bush. Kindly, the driver of the car (another old Land Rover) stopped and asked us about our unfortunate situation. A few explanations were enough for the man to examine the engine. "It seems to be badly burned, we'll try something," he said. He opened his

10. The Price of Water

car, in which I saw several barrels filled with water. He first wet a rag and put it around the alternator or some other part (I forget the name) that was in the engine. He then filled our radiator and said, "Let's go, we'll see if it works! I turned the ignition key and everything started immediately. Never before had I been so happy to hear a car engine start.

Waiting for the return of Gadabak who is looking for water

We restarted it several times to see if it would hold up. When the man saw that it was working, as quickly as he had arrived and without waiting for us, he left with a "have a good trip and be brave." I never found out who the rescuer was, but we thanked the Lord for the help He had sent us.

After another 150 kilometers, we reached Fort Foureau which is now called Kousséri. We arrived just in time to take the last ferry of the day to Ndjamena.

Later, I asked about the problem. The mechanic told me that normally, with an ordinary car, the engine would have been completely ruined. But, probably by a miracle, this one had held up. Well! We experienced two miracles on the same day. My thoughts go to Psalm 60:12: "Through God we shall do valiantly."

The mechanic told me that normally, with an ordinary car, the engine would have been completely ruined. But, probably by a miracle, this one had held up. Well! We experienced two miracles on the same day. My thoughts go to Psalm 60:12: "Through God we shall do valiantly."

11. The Churches that Burn

During our years of service in Cameroon, Mr. Ahmadou Babatoura Ahidjo was President of the Republic. The country gained its independence in January 1960. On May 5, Mr. Ahidjo was elected the first president of the independent country. However, in order to understand what follows, it is important to know that Ahidjo was born in Garoua, a fairly large and important city in the north of the country, located 200 kilometers below Maroua. The north is a Muslim country, mostly inhabited by the Foulani. This is an ethnic group composed of a mixture of West African peoples who have been Islamized for decades. So Ahidjo, as a child from the North, was also a Muslim and naturally an "El Hadji," a name given to all those who made a pilgrimage to Mecca. If I remember correctly, the inhabitants, Christians and Muslims, lived together without any problem. Peace and harmony reigned. But one day, I don't know why, the prefect and the sub-prefect started to make rounds in the villages to force the inhabitants, Catholics and animists, to become Muslims. The chief who did not find ten new converts to Islam within two weeks would be punished with a fine of CFA 10,000, a fortune for these poor people. Everyone was stunned by this injunction and wondered what the reason was. On top of that, they started to burn down the different churches. Why was this? To find out some details, I tried to contact Pastor Menguwé, who wrote to me the following: *"In fact, a certain Monsignor by the name of Ndongmo is said to have ordered a coup d'état against the President of the Republic. Following this affair, the Muslims of the north, belonging to the same religion as the president and with the help of the latter, began to burn down the*

11. The Churches that Burn

Catholic churches in the far north of Cameroon (Ngaoundéré, Garoua, and Maroua). But Adventist churches were not attacked because Adventists were not involved in political affairs." This is one reason why none of our chapels went up in smoke. A second reason why our churches were spared is that it was not the people who were attacked but specifically the church buildings. Soon after the troubles began, the difficulties began to multiply. One after another, Roman churches and then evangelical churches were targeted by arsonists without anything being done. It was expected that it would start soon for our churches. Each of our pastors and the other workers were holding their breath wondering when it would be their turn. A few weeks later, one of our pastors came to me in a hurry. He was carrying good news. People had come to our church to burn it down. But a man in the crowd had suddenly shouted out loud:

> *Often the Sabbath is an obstacle. This time it was a great blessing! Thank you, Lord.*

"Stop, these people are not the same, they don't meet on the same day. They don't go to their churches on Sunday but the day before, on Saturday. They have nothing to do with them!" Suddenly silence returned and the gathering dispersed. Our chapel was spared and no other church elsewhere was threatened. Many other buildings went up in smoke. According to Pastor Amos Menguewé, seventeen Catholic churches were burned or set on fire. I was reminded of one of the words in the Bible that says, "Sanctify my Sabbaths, and let them be a sign between me and you, that you may know that I am the Lord your God" (Ezek. 20: 20). This sign has saved us from many misfortunes and difficulties. Often the Sabbath is an obstacle. This time it was a great blessing! Thank you, Lord.

12. The Cursed Child

One day, very early in the morning, we found a man on the stairs of our house. In his arms, he was carrying a baby of a few months old. The child seemed to be suffering from malnutrition. Strangely enough, he was not at the dispensary waiting for the opening at eight o'clock. No, he wanted to see "Madam" first. In the surrounding villages, my wife is known as "Madam" to everyone. When she started to take care of him, she learned that the mother of this child does not want the baby anymore. For her, he is "cursed," explains the husband in front of us. The child does not eat well, does not gain weight. The father does not know what to do with his child. His wife gave him the child, saying that he was cursed and that she could not do anything with him. She wanted to abandon the baby because she thought that the devil had taken possession of him. So she gave the child to her husband who, of course, did not know how to take care of it. But he didn't believe his wife and wanted to keep his boy at all costs! Totally distraught, he had found no better way than to come to the mission to entrust the child to Madam or at least to help her take care of his son. He was willing to pay for the milk. We already had our two children. My wife didn't think long before coming to the aid of this poor father. We took the child into our home where he slept and ate with our children. Regularly, the man sent or himself brought the milk he had promised. The child began to eat well and gain weight. A few months later, we had to go back to the homeland for furlough. We had to give the child back to his father. How happy he was to see his son back to life! He also had proof for his wife that the child was not cursed! Crazy with joy, a few days later, he came to offer us a calf to express his gratitude. One problem had been solved for us, another one presented itself: what to do with a calf? We quickly decided to give it to the villagers surrounding the mission. To preserve the meat of the calf, I bought some bags of salt with which we coated the animal. This way, the villagers could enjoy it longer.

13. The Twin

During the dry season, we used to sleep on the terrace because of the almost unbearable heat. The terrace was enclosed by a wall about one meter high. On top of this was a fence made of the same material used to fence a chicken coop, to prevent wild animals from jumping onto the terrace. One night we were awakened by a man's voice:

"Madam, Madam come quickly!" Waking up with a start, we inquired about the man's problem. He was from a remote village and said that his

The dispensary in Dogba

wife had given birth to twins but that the women in the village could not get the placenta out after the birth. They had finally decided to seek the intervention of Madam from the clinic. The man set out in the middle of the night to get help. But how to do this with the children and Adelheid, who did not like to drive at night in the bush? We did what we had done the previous time. I offered to go and get the woman in question and bring her to the clinic. My wife would take care of the children and prepare the clinic to receive her.

It's always an experience to move through the bush at night. Fortunately, this time I had a guide who did not get lost in the cotton fields. I don't remember how long I drove but we finally arrived at the village where the woman was waiting for help. I planned to leave with her immediately but the man made me wait in front of a hut that I guessed was his. He had disappeared to who knows where. I had no choice but to wait. Here and there, in a hut, I saw shadows produced by storm lamps, without knowing what was going on. The wait seemed long to me. All I could do was admire the sky. The sky of Africa was such as you cannot see in Europe. With nothing else to do, I admired the celestial panorama, thinking of chapter 37 of the book of Job: "Consider again the wonders of God .... Can you stretch out the heavens as He does?" and Psalm 33:6-13, "The heavens were made by the Word of the Lord... The Lord looks down from heaven, He sees all the sons of men... He watches all the inhabitants of the earth..." I thought about how as God was looking at me, He was also seeing what was going on in the surrounding huts! Finally, after about thirty minutes, the man came back with the woman, accompanied by the village birth attendants. They put her in my car. The man apologized for making me wait. He explained that when he returned, he had discovered that the twins born several hours earlier had not survived and that he still had the painful task of burying them before heading

> *I thought about how as God was looking at me, He was also seeing what was going on in the surrounding huts!*

back with his wife to the clinic to deal with the placenta. The return trip was without further complications. As soon as we arrived, his wife was placed on the examination table at the clinic. Everything was now in darkness, the gloom barely dispelled by the light of a kerosene lamp that I held in my hand. There was no electricity in this lost country and there was no generator at the mission. In the evening, it was dark until the next day at sunrise. Upon further examination, instead of the placenta coming out, another baby saw the light and then another. Both babies were no bigger than my hand, and each weighed around 400 grams. Without an incubator or other instruments suitable for such a situation, the possibility of keeping them alive was almost nil. After the birth of these last two babies, the placenta quickly detached. But the unfortunate parents had no choice but to go home alone the next day, after burying those last two little creatures. I didn't talk much after this adventure, but I thought about Job who said at the beginning of his ordeal: "The Lord gives and the Lord takes away..." There are particularly painful situations where it is difficult to find the right words. This is what I experienced that day.

14. A Day to Never Forget

The day started like any other. However, this one was different: it was the anniversary of our wedding, five years earlier. In other years, we had not taken the time to make it a special day, but this time we planned to celebrate it. Gadabak, a good and honest boy who accompanied me on my rounds[1], also helped us regularly in domestic affairs. It was planned that this 16-year-old orphan would take care of our children for a few hours on that day. This was not new to him and the children liked him. We planned to go to the town of Maroua–town is a big word for a place that was no bigger than a village back home–to do some shopping and eat in a small African restaurant. We left under a blue sky and a burning sun. I don't remember what we bought or what we tasted but what followed marked the rest of our lives! We decided to head back around 3pm. A short hour on the road and we would be home. But as we left Maroua, we noticed clouds in the direction of Dogba. The further we went down the road, the darker the clouds became and soon a torrential downpour totally obscured our view. I have rarely seen such rain. Today, we would probably say it was because of climate change. So much water fell from the sky that we had to stop to avoid slipping or being swept away in canyons formed by the rainfall. The water washes away everything in its path. It's amazing how rains can form giant canyons.

    What can happen in a few hours gives you an idea of what can happen when water falls in great quantities for forty days and forty nights, as it is

---

[1]See chapter, "The Price of Water."

The power and work of water

written in Genesis, at the time of the flood. Add earthquakes caused by volcanic explosions and you can see that the account in Genesis 7 is not exaggerated at all. No, neither the Grand Canyon in the USA, nor the Bryce Canyon, needed millions of years to form!

After a short moment of calm, we very carefully followed our path because, once in a crevasse, you have difficulty to get out or you risk being swept away by the waters! And here, to understand the rest of the story, I have to tell a little bit about the history of the Dogba Adventist Mission.

It was in the 1930s that our brother Bergström arrived in Cameroon to begin missionary work in the north of the country, among the Kirdi. They were a people very resistant to any foreign influence. The Muslims had already tried to Islamize them, but without success. From the start, the authorities advised Bergström against working among them, "wasted work," he was told. *One government official said that he felt very sorry for the missionaries. "We have never succeeded in doing anything for these people," he said, "and we doubt whether you will be able to evangelize such wild men.*

14. A Day to Never Forget

The power of water again

Even though you stay here for fifty years you will never see progress among these tribes!" Fortunately, he proved mistaken.[2]

It is also important to know that the village of Dogba has always been divided into two parts by the marigot (a kind of channel that is dry most of the year but fills up very quickly once the rains come). On one side of the channel lived the Muslims, on the other side our missionary Bergström who had decided to establish the mission among the pagans in order to better reach them and perhaps also to avoid being "persona non grata" among the Muslims. The only problem was that it was necessary to be able to go out by car during the rainy season. The temporary passage that crossed the marigot was always washed away in the rainy season. Bergström decided to buy a small plot of land near the channel on the other side, on the Muslim side, to build a shed and put his car there during that

---

[2**] This information was taken from the missionary report of August 21, 1965, written by Bergström.

time of the year so that he could always leave if necessary. To get to this car-port, after the rain, one could usually walk across.

I now return to my story. As we continued our way through the crevasses and canyons, both old and new, we began to discuss and imagine what condition we would find the Wadi (channel) at the mission after this heavy rain. How would we reach the house and the children? The temporary passage would surely be washed away... Finally, we arrived at Dogba. We drove our "all-terrain" vehicle into the shed and saw, right in front of us, a wadi in spectacular flooding. Impossible to cross on foot. We considered our options. Would we wait here for hours for the water to recede or, being young and good swimmers, would we swim to the other side? Seeing us in the face of this water, which in its force was carrying a lot of mud and debris from the surrounding mountains, the Muslim villagers with whom we had a very good relationship crowded around us, strongly advising us against diving into the swirling water to try to reach the other side. On the "mission" shore, the locals, most of them Christians, also arrived quickly to see what we were going to do. Several shouted messages to us. But the current was so noisy that we could not understand what they meant. It seemed to us that everyone wanted to warn us of a danger that we did not know. We were good swimmers in our eyes and none of the spectators could swim, but we could! So, sure of ourselves, we started to swim. However, once in the water, we quickly realized that we should have listened to the good advice of the spectators on both sides. The current was so strong that we were not able to swim very fast and we were in danger of being swept away by the rushing current. And what strength it took to be able to swim!

The current was so strong that we were not able to swim very fast and we were in danger of being swept away by the rushing current.

Soon, Adelheid was swept away by the current even more than I was. In these torrential waters, her skirt made the effect of a sail in which the current of water gained in energy. We encouraged each other but I quickly found myself at the end of my strength. When I finally reached the shore, some of the brothers came to me and pulled me up onto dry land. I saw from a distance my dear wife who was still struggling to reach the shore as I was, but she was swept further away by the current. I was now dry and with the strength I had left, I ran after her along the river. I didn't have enough strength left to jump in the water to help her. I only had the energy to shout words of encouragement to her. Finally, after struggling against the force of the water, she shouted to me, "I can't take it anymore! I can't take it anymore!" She raised her hand to bid me farewell and let herself go to disappear into the turbulent waters. At that very moment, what no one could believe happened. There was a sand bank there and instead of being swept away and disappearing into the swirling waters, she found herself, unpredictably, standing on that bank in the middle of the swamp. From that moment, without thinking, our African brothers who had followed our swim with astonishment and fear, jumped one after the other into the water, without thinking of the risks and dangers for themselves. They made a chain with their hands to help the shipwrecked woman and bring her to land. After this adventure, we went home and thanked the Lord on our knees for this heavenly intervention. We were able to experience God's words from Isaiah 43:2: "When you pass through the waters, I will be with you; and when you pass through the rivers, they will not sweep over you" (NIV).

> *For me, that day is marked as THE day God saved my wife and gave her to me for the second time.*

For me, that day is marked as *THE* day God saved my wife and gave her to me for the second time. The first time being our marriage. I use the words "second time" on purpose because another one will follow later.

15. Old Man David

Many other stories come to mind when my mind goes back to the past. The years go by so fast that we are in danger of forgetting, yet so many things have gradually shaped our lives and our character... I could write more pages about the years spent in Dogba. Before talking about our next destinations, I must add this one.

A few months had passed at the station. One Sabbath in church, we had Communion Service. An old man was in the front pews, right in front of me while I was officiating for the Communion Service. Before the service, I had already been introduced to him as the chief deacon of the church. He was sitting in front of me, dressed in a slightly scruffy shirt, an old jacket, shorts, and some kind of old moccasins, well aware of the sacred service and his responsibility to pass on the bread and the cup. I could say that if one had to choose a saint in the church, it would surely have been him! Another deacon was sitting next to him, a brother who, to my knowledge, was consecrated and dedicated to the task for which he had been chosen. The preaching service, the washing of the feet and the distribution of the bread had gone well, we were at

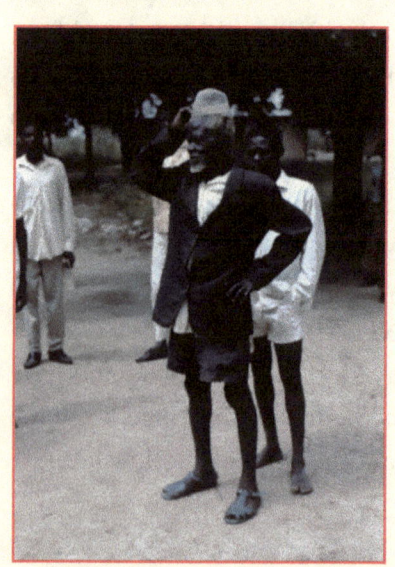

The first Kirdi convert after 15 years, "Old Man David"

the service of the cup. Since we did not have individual glasses, the deacons passed between the rows with a large cup from which each participant drank a sip.

As usual, they came back with the rest and gave me the cup so that I could give it to them and they could drink in turn. With this intention, I gave our old deacon David a cup that was still one-third full, which he received with thanks and began to drink the rest. In all kindness, I almost had to snatch the cup from his hands to still have the opportunity to serve the other deacon and myself. I should also mention that he was not near the table and I had to rush from behind the serving table to retrieve the remaining juice. When I saw this scene unfold before my eyes, I had to make a real effort not to burst out laughing.

After the service, one of the brothers came to me and told me a little bit about the story of David. (We had the privilege of visiting Brother Bergström a few years later in Sweden and he told us exactly the same thing about old David.) When Ruben Bergström, in the 1930's, came to settle on this side of the swamp, as I said above, it was with the intention of being closer to the Kirdi. The news of the missionary's arrival among the Kirdi provoked great curiosity, and Bergström began a meeting every Sabbath under a mango tree in the field. David, the chief of his tribe, came with his guards and many other people from his village to listen to what the white man had to tell them. Bergström's wife, who was a nurse, took care of their patients during the week. Isn't it written somewhere that the right arm of the gospel is medical work? It was also in this context that the dispensary at the station was established. Sabbath after Sabbath, David came to hear the message of the gospel. This was repeated for fifteen years, after which David was the first member to be baptized among the Kirdi. I wonder if Ruben Bergström ever intended to give up preaching. It seems that he was a man of patience,

> *When I saw this scene unfold before my eyes, I had to make a real effort not to burst out laughing.*

and his patience paid off in the end. Fifteen years of waiting for the first baptism! Many others have followed since then and Dogba has become a great mission station, which today has a college called Bergström College in memory of the tireless work of the man who had so much patience and so much love to tell the love of Jesus.

16. The Locusts

Not far from our house, there was a kind of oasis, something exceptional in this arid place. It was like a green patch in the desert.

The moisture in the ground never dried up. Even when the marsh was completely dry, and the villagers had to dig for water, it was guaranteed. One or two mango trees grew there. My wife had planted a small vegetable garden there, which provided us from time to time with fresh vegetables such as salads, carrots, a few tomatoes and radishes. Adelheid,

The marigot/channel of Dogba in dry season

with our help from home, regularly went to see what we could harvest. We had plenty of onions around the house. They were watered daily. But one day a boy came running to the house, "Pastor, locusts, locusts!" I didn't immediately understand what he meant. But, between breaths, he added, "Locusts are eating your vegetables!" I immediately went to look, but what could I do? I had no way to chase the locusts away or stop them from eating the vegetables. When we arrived a little later, the damage was already done. Most of the garden looked like another desert in the middle of the desert. The mango trees still had some foliage. Everything else we could forget. We must have had some of the feeling that Pharaoh must have had after the eighth plague in Exodus 10. To prevent such a disaster from happening again, we only continued to grow onions around the house, adding garlic and tomatoes. These crops were always richly blessed and we remembered that, after all, the Israelites never lacked onions and garlic either.

17. Projects Come to Life

We should not forget that our hospital in Koza was located about 100 kilometers from Dogba. Occasionally, the doctor who was on duty at the hospital, and who also had a very busy schedule, would visit the dispensary.

Doubtful cases and people who needed a more thorough examination for an accurate diagnosis were presented to him. During our stay, it was Dr. Kohlia Stéveny. During this time, another missionary also arrived in Koza: Franz Krakolinig. We always had a pleasant collaboration and it was

The first dormitory of Dogba College

The first students in front of the dormitory

also the Krakolinig family who replaced us after our departure and continued to develop the college. A small dormitory was financed by a donor from the Belgian-Luxembourg Conference (in the picture, the small dormitory and the first students). My brother Franz had the privilege of building two classroom buildings after our departure with the financial help of European donors.

This was done in 1972 and 1973. Bergström College was finally created by my successor Franz Krakolinig. For the official opening of the college in 1973, Brother Bergström was invited and stayed for 2 weeks. It was a great moment! (This last information was given to me by the Krakolinig family who, in turn, returned to their homeland in 1974).

Before leaving the North of Cameroon, I must also remind you that it was during these years that the land for the church in Garoua and the plot in Maroua were also purchased. This last plot was bought from a Lebanese who was about to return to his country. So my thoughts go back to the beginning of the church in N'Gaoundéré. The few members who were in that city had asked me to visit them. There were no permanent workers there yet. I went there to find about ten people gathered that Sabbath morning. In Garoua, we had a brother who had been sent by the Union to develop the work begun there. We were meeting in the house of our young evangelist, whose name I have forgotten. I went there regularly to assist the members in their daily struggle. By the way, we should not forget that it was (and still is) a Muslim country. One Sabbath morning after the service, a brother came to see me. He was having problems with his boss regarding having the Sabbath off and he asked me if I could intervene. The next day I went to see his boss. It was an opportunity to give a study on the Sabbath, at the end of which our brother got his Sabbath off on condition that he make up the Sabbath hours during the week. The Adventist church has grown at a remarkable rate in this city. We soon had in view a beautiful piece of land on which to locate our chapel and possibly other buildings. The plans became a reality a few months later. I still remember spending several days there with Brother R. Colin, treasurer of the Union at that time, to finalize the purchase. The figures I received recently indicate that there are 5,378 members in N'Gaoundéré and 6,118 in Garoua. There are even 30,025 in Maroua and its surroundings. When I look at and count the beginnings of evangelism in these cities and their regions, I can only marvel and give glory to God. I can say with Paul: "I (we) planted the seed, Apollos watered it, but God has been making it grow," (1 Cor. 3:6, NIV). I don't know who bought the land in N'Gaoundéré or who gave the mandate. This must have happened after I left. The distance between these three cities was not negligible and was about 500 kilometers.

18. After

After these blessed and tumultuous years in the North of the country, the end of our stay in Dogba was approaching. I had asked the union and the division to return to the mainland to continue my studies. For this purpose, I had chosen the University of London where I could take correspondence courses. Meanwhile, I was assigned to the Belgian-Luxembourg Conference to continue the evangelistic work in the Grand Duchy of Luxembourg. Based on the tithe receipts found in the archives of the Friedensau Seminary of the German Union, the Adventist work in this country dates back to 1907. All traces are lost after this date. The following documents date back to the 1930s. During this time, a certain Brother Klamm came there to meet with some members. In 1968, the territory of Luxembourg was attached to the Belgian Conference. And at the same time, Brother Fernand Lecompte started to follow up on the addresses collected after the conferences held by Brother Lanarès in the city of Luxembourg. I received a few addresses from these two brothers to get started.

Concerning my studies, I soon encountered difficulties at the conference offices that I can describe as a lack of organization or information between the conference and the division. When the division would send me a check to participate in the purchase of study books that I needed, our conference was not at all of the same mind. I had to work in evangelism and nothing else, otherwise I could go to Switzerland to get my salary. As a result, my studies progressed very slowly. The number of times I went to London was reduced to the bare minimum. The work of evangelization was not going smoothly. I was mainly doing door-to-door outreach. It was hard work that did not always produce the desired result. In a country that was known to be more Catholic than the Pope, I was chased away many times, as if I had been a beggar. Once, I even had a dog sent after me. But on occasion, people have shown some interest in the Word of God and have even let me into their homes. For example, one very interested lady allowed me to come back for regular studies until... One morning, someone rang my doorbell. When I opened it, I was confronted by a rather portly gentleman. "Are you Mr. Cools?" he asked me in a somewhat aggressive tone. When I answered in the affirmative, he continued in a loud voice: "Leave my wife alone! I don't want you to come over to the house for your Bible study anymore, whether you like it or not! Thank you!" He turned his back on me and left. To this day, I could never figure out how he found our address. I never gave it out and it was not in the phone book because there was no phone line available in the village where we lived. In case of an emergency, we had to make arrangements with the neighbors. It is important to note that we lived in a village about 40 kilometers from the capital city of Luxembourg. It was not easy to get there by public transport, buses being rare in those days.

During those years I received the visit of some colleagues who came to help me in the door-to-door work. They came to encourage me and I am still very grateful for their support!

At the time we arrived, the church was composed of about ten members scattered throughout the country. Each of them had their own history and had become Adventists in a particular way. Very briefly, apart from the conferences of the two brothers mentioned above, the group had started for the third time with a German Adventist who had settled in Luxembourg after the Second World War and who had started to talk to anyone who wanted to know something about our message. The few members who formed our group always supported me faithfully in every way. Some of them were even willing to accompany me in the door-to-door work.

About a year and a half later, we received a letter from Brother E. Ludescher, president of the union in Yaoundé, asking us if we would be willing to return to Cameroon. Another brother (whose name I have forgotten) working in the West of Cameroon, more precisely in Buea, was about to leave and had no intention of returning. They had to find an evangelist and a nurse again. We had not been forgotten by the original union. Soon Brother Ludescher, who was on leave, came to visit us and talk to us. I remember that his first remark was: "Ihr lebt da wo Hase und Fux sich begegnen" which means: "You live in such a secluded corner that the fox and the rabbit can easily meet here without being disturbed." The reason for this isolation was the low rent, which was much more expensive elsewhere and the conference was not willing to pay more. After our meeting, my wife and I were a little relieved to leave this country that was not very open to the gospel.

Each of the few members had also experienced their own ordeal. To give an idea of the religious situation at that time, here is one of their stories. The brother in question (I withhold his name for the sake of discretion) was disabled and received a small disability pension. When he no longer showed up at the Roman church for Sunday mass or confession, the priest came to visit his parishioner to find out the reason for his absence. They soon began a discussion about the day of rest. The priest, not knowing what to say, accused our brother of joining a cult. "You are a sect," he accused. To which our brother very calmly replied: "Ah, you say that we are a sect, but I will show you who you are." And opening his Bible in Matthew 23: 9, our brother read: "...call no one on earth your father, for only one is your Father, he who is in heaven," to which he quietly added: "You see, we can call no one father, and you even have a Holy Father." The priest was furious and, again not knowing what to say to this, he asked if our brother was indeed disabled and received his monthly disability pension from the state pension fund, to which the latter retorted: "But what business is that of yours?" The vicar got up and left the house, leaving our brother to wonder about this last question of the priest. He would soon understand. At the end of the month, his disability pension did not arrive and this lasted for several years. The priest wanted to show him who was the strongest. Our brother had to go to court for years to have his disability recognized again. At that time, it was: "The State is the Church and the Church is the State." Fortunately, those days are over, but other problems remain.

I must say, however, that during our work in this country, which was not very open to the Gospel, and before we left again for Cameroon, God blessed this small community with a few baptisms, either through the door-to-door work or through some children of church members. Two years later, we left again for a few years in Cameroon, this time assigned to Buea. Another chapter begins.

19. At Mount Cameroon

You will soon understand the title of this chapter. We were met at the airport in Douala by Brother K. Scheidegger. After spending the night at his place, he showed us around Douala, after which we left for Buea, some seventy kilometers away from Douala. The city lies at an altitude of about 1000 meters and is the capital of the southwest region with English as the main language, but also the "pidgin" dialect. The Adventist church was established there only a few years ago. It started with the establishment

Mount Cameroon

of a dispensary known as "Seventh-day," separate from the local hospital which lacked most of the necessary facilities.

The good care and medicines of Seventh-day were known far and wide. The dispensary received many visits. Buea is a city at the foot of Mount Cameroon as I said, at an altitude of 1000 meters, which has a non-tropical climate. Life is pleasant here, but in the evening it is cool. Mount Cameroon is almost always in the clouds, but on the days when it was visible, we had a magnificent view. Our house was on the hill a few kilometers from the dispensary. My wife started to give care right away and I went to discover the places where the different churches and groups were located. I was now often accompanied by Brother Godefroy Mubélé. I cannot fail to mention his name. He was a man who had evangelism in his heart and without him, I would not have known how to proceed. He knew how to easily find the most remote churches or groups that I could not find. We mustn't forget that GSM and GPS didn't exist yet in those days. It was not easy to understand people at the beginning either. Pidgin is not a common English but it is a deformed English that was developed during the colonial period. You should know that a negative sentence is always positive. Let's take an example. When we say "I come," the man on the spot will say: "I don't come" or for "I go" he will say "I don't go." I have to say that at first I had a hard time getting into it. Our children were taught at home by a kind teacher provided by the union.

From time to time I had to go to Victoria, a port city which is now called "Limbe." We had an evangelist worker there who was working hard to start a church there. "Udo" was from Nigeria, a young boy dedicated to his work. We decided to conduct an evangelistic campaign. For this purpose, the local authorities had put a community hall at our disposal. Invitations and large posters were printed by our printing house in Yaoundé, which we distributed with the help of the few members on site. The result exceeded all our expectations. People arrived in droves and the community hall was soon too small to hold everyone. Chairs were in short supply and even the standing room was filled. The attendance was the same every night. After two weeks of campaigning, on Friday night we invited people to come on Sabbath morning to visit our little church, which was nothing more than a large room in Udo's house. Our prayers were answered. About ten people showed up. At the end of the service, a gentleman stood up and asked if he could ask a question.

"Gentlemen, you've told us a lot of things that we think are true, that's why we're here. Only you've created a problem for us. What do we do now? We have to work on Saturday and thanks to your talks we now know that it is the day of the Lord Jesus and that we should observe it instead of Sunday. What should we do?" I knew he was a man who worked in a state ministry. Udo and I were taken by surprise. After a moment of silence, I answered him: "Yes sir, I am aware that we have created a problem for you, but I cannot hold back the Word of God either. Unfortunately, I cannot help you any further and it is now up to you to act by trusting in the Word of Him who saved us. To our amazement, he attended the following Sabbaths at church services happy to have found a truth he had never dared to think about. He soon told us that he had asked his boss for his Sabbath and that his boss had granted it to him without much difficulty. Udo continued to teach our friend, who was then baptized in the sea. Shortly thereafter, the brother was assigned to Bamenda, and we to Douala to replace the Scheideggers. Unfortunately, I was not able to follow the journey of our brother Makkias, which I think was his name. But a few years later, I learned that he had remained a good church member, still working in the Bamenda municipal administration and free to observe the Sabbath.

The time spent in the West was also rich in experiences. It is always a joy and a grace to see people give themselves to the Lord. One day, Udo told me that he had prepared a person interested in baptism.[3] A Sabbath

---

[3] I don't know if it was as a result of the conferences, but it doesn't matter here.

19. At Mount Cameroon

The church in Buea

was set aside so that after the service we could go to the sea where the baptism would take place.

As usual it was a beautiful day, except that the sea was rough. Once in the water, the waves that were rising and falling lifted me up with such force that neither the candidate nor I had regular footing. We had to wait for the right moment between two waves. They came so fast that I could not immerse the candidate. After the baptismal formula and at the right moment, the candidate was immersed, but then a wave propelled us upwards and neither of us had a foothold yet and we were carried further out to sea by the force of the water. When the water receded, a new trough fortunately formed and we regained our footing. We quickly got out of the sea before another wave swept us further out to sea. The assembly gathered on the beach sang heartily, I suppose to give thanks that two candidates were baptized! The second one was obviously not planned—it was me! After such an event, we had to laugh a little. It was a baptism like no other!

Another event marked my ministry during 1974. It happened during an evangelistic campaign in Kumba. Kumba is a city seventy kilometers from Buea and is very commercial. Palm oil and cocoa are the mainstay of its trade. In those days, it must have had about 80,000 inhabitants. A large market was part of daily life. We decided to conduct an evangelization campaign there. In the city itself, we had a small building as a church, well situated on a main axis crossing the city. The printing house in Yaoundé had again delivered the invitations and the posters on which was written: "Come and listen to God and palaver" (the pidgin for "come and listen to the Word of God"). A week-long campaign was planned, with each lecture translated into pidgin each evening. There were no crowds like in Victoria, but people did come to listen. We soon noticed that each night a gentleman was listening with intense interest and always sitting in the same seat in the front row. The night I spoke about the Sabbath, he came up to us after the meeting. He said, "Thank you for this message. I found what I'm looking for!" he said. And he told us part of his story. As a shopkeeper, he had a large store in the market. Reading his Bible, he had come to the conclusion that Sunday is not the day established by God but that the Sabbath, or Saturday, should be. Subsequently, he decided to close his store on Saturdays and held a service with his family in his house, waiting to discover a Sabbath-keeping church. This was not the only subject he was interested in, but also the return of Jesus, death as sleep, and other things he had discovered in his Bible! Who says that there is no more interest among the people of the world who honestly seek God? Shortly afterwards, he was baptized.

Buea was the place for evangelistic campaigns. One of the last ones was conducted in Tiko. I think it was in 1973. Like all the others, the city

The assembly gathered on the beach sang heartily, I suppose to give thanks that two candidates were baptized! The second one was obviously not planned—it was me!

19. At Mount Cameroon

The current dispensary in Buea

of Tiko in the seventies was not what it is today. The same goes for Buea, Kumba, or Douala. Time has not stood still. Today there are about 130,000 inhabitants, in 1973 there were maybe 70,000 or 100,000. I don't remember exactly, but I still remember the campaign to bring the Gospel there. The municipality lent us a hall again. The invitations and posters always came from our printing house in Yaoundé. The hall was full to capacity.

After one or two weeks,[4] our local evangelist had collected a lot of addresses to give studies and visit people. The reason I remember this campaign well is that a few weeks later a fire destroyed a large part of the city. Unfortunately, there is nothing about this in the 1973 archives of the city of Tiko. The archives did not yet exist in those years and it seems to me that this catastrophic fire has been forgotten. Today we only remember the market fire that took place in 2010. I am talking about 1973. The situation was so serious at that time that I pleaded with the union and

---

[4] I have lost my memory of that.

the division to send exceptional aid for the reconstruction of Tiko. This request was heard and the division in Bern sent us a check, in the amount of CFA 400,000, if I remember correctly, which was a nice sum at that time. My brother Mubélé and I had the joy and the privilege of giving this check to the city authorities who were delighted with this unexpected help. There are many more things I could tell you about those years in West Cameroon.

But in 1975, we were called to Douala to replace the Scheideggers who had reached the end of their term of office to be assigned to Batouri, 600 kilometers to the east. Brother and Sister Giger, who had already served for a few years in Zima, CAR, came to replace us in Buea. It is worth mentioning here that since the modest beginnings in Buea with the dispensary, a modern hospital, also called health center, with 33 beds has been added. The picture on the right shows the current facility; on the left, the original dispensary from the 1970s is still visible. The fence did not yet exist. It was also during these years that the church in Buea was built, which needed a dignified meeting place for the growing number of members.

20. Douala

The mission in Douala was in the middle of the city, in the Bali district, where I know it is still located today. Our children needed a school, which was another reason for our move. They went to the French school Dominique Savio.

My territory was also extended from Kribi in the south to Dschang and Bafoussam, Foumban in the French-speaking west, plus the whole English-speaking west, Buea, Kumba, Bamenda, without forgetting the attendance at the big church in Douala with all its worries. Fortunately, I had the help of Mario Giger in the English-speaking territory. We were often on the road together and encouraged each other in the face of daily challenges.

The place I had to visit most often was Kribi because we had a college there (simply called "the college of Kribi"). It was always a very tiring trip on a road that was only paved between Douala and Edea but was not easily passable because of large potholes. One had to be extremely careful. In addition, the tar had often been completely removed on large stretches. As soon as we passed Edea,

The road between Edea and Kribi

the so-called tar was finished, and we still had about 125 kilometers to go to Kribi. This part of the road, which was a main artery, was more of a simple bush track. Bush trucks and cabs (always overloaded) often turned the road into a big quagmire. Anyway, once we left Douala, driving the 200 kilometers to Kribi was always an adventure! I have since learned that the road situation has improved tremendously.

Here are three events on that journey that I can't forget. One day, in the middle of the rainy season, Scheidegger suggested that I go by road to Edea to visit and introduce myself to some of the stations. Even during the rains, the road to Edea was passable without too many problems. However, after driving about 60 kilometers, we came across a huge quagmire, one of those places where the tar had been completely washed away over the years. On both sides of the road, cabs, trucks, and as many private cars were blocked by trucks and other vehicles that blocked the entire passage. On both sides, on the banks extending the road, a multitude of villagers were talking without moving. Occasionally, they would move to help someone out by pushing with all their might. We soon realized that the passage was possible for whoever was willing to put out some money. Those who could not afford it or did not want to empty their pockets were stuck. We were among those who searched their pockets. For the pastors, the price was cheaper because they prayed for them! Two days later, we learned that after the arrival of the authorities, the famous quagmire had to be filled in by the villagers who had dug it to create a small source of income. Clever thinking!

The second event I remember is the following. I had to go to Kribi—I don't know exactly why. Apart from the college, we also had an elementary school there with about 100 students and quite a large number of members with a permanent church that was under construction at that time. But the reason for my visit is not relevant here. It should be mentioned that it was in the middle of the rainy season and I did not want to take any risk with my personal car. That's why I had chosen to go there by bush cab where we were squeezed like in a sardine can. During the trip, the passengers had already had to get out several times to lighten the combi and push to get through the huge quagmires that had formed. We finally arrived in Kribi. I stayed there for several days in a kind of hotel room that was not four stars but rather "minus four stars." But that doesn't matter much. After doing what I had come for, I had to find a way to get home. Bush cabs were scarce because the trip was risky. I started looking early in the morning and luck was with me. I found an opportunity. The departure was scheduled for the evening. The trip would take place during the night. I found this a little strange because you can see better in the daylight. But the main thing was that I had found a vehicle to return. I wanted to pay right away to make sure I had my seat at night. "No, no, your name is on my list and you will be sitting in the front." Sitting in the front is already an advantage, not in case of an accident, but it is surely a bit more comfortable than being squeezed like sardines on the benches in the back. In the evening, around 7 pm, all the travelers were present to start the expedition to Douala. The difficult passages being well known, we advanced slowly. There was only bush to the left and to the right. Occasionally, a hut with the faint light of a storm lamp could be seen. Suddenly, in the middle of the journey between Kribi and Edea, in the middle of nature, the driver stopped. We were all told to get out of the cab because we were going to have to pay up. We were asked to pay exorbitant amounts of money. Everyone understood the driver's game. Whoever did not pay could spend the night in the jungle.

> *We were all told to get out of the cab because we were going to have to pay up. We were asked to pay exorbitant amounts of money. Everyone understood the driver's game. Whoever did not pay could spend the night in the jungle.*

Of course, all kinds of words and insults were hurled at the driver, but no matter what the objections or insults were, the one who doesn't pay stays. One hour later, the business concluded, we left again. Finally, after hours that seemed interminable, we arrived at the city gate of Douala. You never enter the city at night without having passed the police checkpoints and our driver was at great risk of being fined for overloading with passengers. The solution: 1 kilometer before we arrived at the checkpoint, half of the passengers had to get off and walk through the police checkpoints after the cab had passed. One kilometer after the checkpoint, the driver waited again for all the passengers to continue the journey through the city to the bus station. It was three o'clock in the morning when I arrived home. I thought of Psalm 121:8 "The Lord will keep your going and your coming...." Praise God!

The third trip to Kribi to remember is the one below. I often went there for different reasons. This time, in the middle of the dry season, we had decided that I would take the children. I took the opportunity to spend one or two days with them at the beautiful beach of Kribi. I had included these days of relaxation with them in my program. A kind of vacation with the children. From two trips, we made one. Already days before the trip,

The beach at Kribi

Heidi and Ben were delighted to go on a tour with "daddy," especially at the beach in Kribi.

My wife could not join us because since we moved to Douala, she had found a job at the clinic of Dr. Ekanda, a cardiologist, not far from our house. What I must mention here is that every time I went to the bush, I had the car loaded with equipment. The road between Douala and Edea was, as I wrote earlier, full of potholes. To avoid them, you almost have to drive in zigzags, but doing so at full speed is almost impossible. So we drove at a reduced speed. At one point, a tire got a flat. A stop to change it was necessary. Once on the road again, I drove with the hope of arriving safely in Edea to have the flat tire repaired because there was no place to repair it before we got there.

Edea is an industrial town known for its aluminum production. That's where I could find a garage or a gas station. The town is one of the few crossing points for the Sanaga River between Douala and Yaoundé. The old iron bridge had a single lane on which vehicles, trains, and pedestrians passed. I don't know if the situation is still the same. It doesn't matter!

What I feared happened about 50 kilometers from the city. A second tire broke and the worst thing that could happen: at the moment when I stop because of this second puncture, a third tire, the front left one, broke as well. We have one spare tire but not three! We are now in a very painful situation! A car full of goods, two small children (eight and six years old), a suffocating heat, and three flat tires. I usually have the materials to fix it. But I assure you, fixing two or three tubes is no small task! We were most likely going to spend the rest of the day there. Seeing our desperate situation (and the two little ones seemed to realize it), we called for help from above. We prayed for Jesus to send us help. The road was not very busy for a main road. A few bush cabs passed by, but they did so at high speed because for them, every minute lost represents less money earned at the end of the day. Apart from these already overloaded and time-pressed vehicles, there was indeed little traffic but our wait was not in vain. A vehicle stopped and a nice man offered to take us to Edea. That was enough, but I still had a problem and a huge responsibility. Could I leave my car, full of goods for the college and the workers, for who knows how long without supervision? What would I find next? It wouldn't be the first time that an unattended car was emptied, or even that an entire vehicle disappeared into the bush, to be sold for spare parts at a market here or there. I had already talked to the kids about the possibility that they would have to be the guardians during a possible absence of Dad. We had been praying and Jesus would surely be by their side. The decisive moment had now arrived. I was confident that the Lord would watch over my children and the car. One more big kiss to each of them, along with the final instructions not to walk away from Daddy's car, and I left with the nice man. I drove away with a heavy heart, silently praying that God would keep my children. We arrived an hour later in Edea. On the way, I worried about how I would get back to the breakdown site with two tires and how I would find the children. It seemed a little later that these worries were unjustified because the man who had picked me up along the way quickly found a gas station and said, reassuringly, "And how will you get back? Don't worry, I'll wait here with you to take you back." At that moment, it was like a big stone that fell from my heart. An hour later, once the punctures were fixed, we were off again. How are my two little ones? We arrived and there they were, proud of their job as watchdogs. A few cars had stopped, asking the children what they were doing there, all alone. "Our daddy, the pastor, went to fix the car's tires" was their reply. With the pedestrians, the discussion was a little longer and they were able to give testimony of their faith, that Jesus was watching over Daddy's car with them!

The person who had picked me up and brought me back then went back to Edea. I quickly put the tires back on, after which we continued our journey to Edea and Kribi without further incident. We could not stop thanking the Lord. I thought and still think about Psalm 18: 31, 32 which says:

"With my God, I cross a wall. The ways of God are perfect. The Word of the Lord is tried and tested; He is a shield for all who trust in Him!" Thank you Lord, you are truly great!

21. Oubenicam

This was at the time when Mario Giger had replaced me in Buea. In the meantime, a request had arrived from a remote group of members of a certain place known as Oubenicam. This place has another name today and is now called something like Kumbo and Demari. The church there required Communion Service. The place had the name I mentioned. I don't remember if it was an islet or a peninsula off the coast of West Cameroon or the name of a village on an island. In any case, the only way to get there was by boat. On a Friday morning, we set off. We had to pass the town of Kumba and from there we headed for a mangrove where, during high tide, a fairly large boat could dock. The boat was already there when we arrived and a crowd was waiting patiently to board. But before the passengers boarded, the hold had to be filled with goods for the local population of Oubenicam. I was surprised to see how much beer was part of the cargo. We had to leave our car there, hoping to find it on Sunday evening. Finally, when everything was put away and the passengers in their places, it was time to leave with an overloaded boat, hoping that we would arrive at the right port, which was the case after several hours, first through the mangrove to finally go to the open sea, a rather rough sea. Upon our arrival, we were cordially received by our brothers and sisters who led us through the narrow streets of the village to our temporary home during our stay. There we had several meetings with the members as well as many individual visits with people who were more animist. Everywhere we were warmly received. The only problem we experienced was on the last night. That night, it rained heavily and the roof of the hut where we were staying was eaten away by termites to such an extent that nothing remained dry inside. Thus, our beds and all our equipment were soaked and we did not sleep a wink all night. Fortunately, that was the last night. The next morning, we had another farewell meeting during which we implored God's grace on his work in this place so cut off from the rest of the world. After the blessed days there, we made our way back in the same boat we had arrived in. We found our car in place and had every reason to thank the Lord not only for keeping our vehicle but for protecting and blessing us during this unusual trip. We were very happy to be back with our respective families and to eat something other than fish, the main food of Oubenicam. I recall here Psalm 133:1: "How good and pleasant it is when God's people live together in unity!" (NIV).

22. Blocked on the Road

The road between Douala, Nkongsamba, and Bafoussam was a paved road and regularly maintained, so there were not too many potholes. But once you left this road to go to a village a little far from the main road, it was often hell. So, I once had to go to one of these villages to spend the weekend with one or more bush churches, I don't remember exactly. I have also forgotten the name of the village where I was to end up. Our Brother Makong André, who often accompanied me to these places far from my territory, had already left several days in advance to prepare the assembly and I knew the place. It was in the rainy season, but since most of the route was paved, I was not worried. How wrong I was! After leaving the main road, the misery began. The track was very narrow and full of holes in which one could easily get stuck. That Friday night, it seemed to me that the trip was endless. The day slowly started to decline, yet I was still hoping to arrive at the destination village to join the beginning of the Sabbath in the church under the banana leaf roof. But suddenly, about 30 kilometers from my destination, I saw a large truck blocking my way. It was so bogged down that it absolutely needed help to get out of it. I couldn't go left or right if I didn't want to risk complicating my situation. I got out, went around the vehicle a few times, yelled to see if the driver was anywhere, honked the horn a few times but nothing, no sign of life! I didn't know if the vehicle had been stuck here for several days or since the morning itself. There was no way for me to turn around and go back the other way. And backing up seemed more than a feat. What to do? For once I didn't have a brother on board to accompany me, I was in a really bad situation. The only consolation was that even with a co-pilot, there wasn't much we could have done about it! Now the other animals living in the bush seemed to say "good evening" to me, still accompanied by the noise of the crickets and locusts that filled the cacophony of the bush surrounding me and that seemed to say "see you tomorrow." All that remained was to settle down in my car to spend the night, hoping that tomorrow morning... I listened to some more of the beautiful music on my tapes and at the end, of course, I said my prayer "Lord, it's yours now and you know that they are waiting for me tomorrow morning, your Holy Day, in your house." Very quiet and confident, I fell asleep. The mobile phone was not yet available to warn André of my situation. Oh, how the world has changed!

What I didn't know was that at the other end of the road that night, seeing that I wasn't arriving, the church members prayed late into the night that the Lord would protect me and that I would at least make it to the Sabbath service. It's kind of like the story of Peter and the church in Acts 12. Everyone prays on their own side of the obstacle. It seems from the reading of Acts that Peter was sleeping peacefully while the church

was praying for God to remove the obstacle. There are situations where you can do nothing but trust. This was my case! I also slept peacefully, as did Peter. I woke up the next day around six o'clock with the sunrise. I couldn't believe my eyes when I didn't see a truck anymore! The vehicle had disappeared, without me having heard or seen anything. But one thing was certain: someone had come to take the truck away. I never knew who it was or how it happened. But I thanked God for the removal of this obstacle and without delay, I continued on my way. After a good hour, I arrived at the village where the church was waiting for me. There I was told about the night of prayer that this church had held for my safe arrival. Songs and thanksgiving went up to heaven that Sabbath morning and I can still say today, "Thank you Lord for hearing our prayers that night." "I call on you, my God, for you will answer me" (Ps. 17:6, NIV).

It would be unfair to forget to mention other brothers who have been close collaborators and have assisted me with their precious advice and help which I have always greatly appreciated. Among them was Etollo Bem Daniel, who served as a pastor in the vicinity of the city of Douala. During every trip to Kribi,[5] he was there to assist me with all the translations and unexpected events that could occur. There was also Pastor Makong André, the one who was far away in the vicinity of Djang and Kongsamba, and Brother Mongo Jean-Claude who was directly in charge of the church in Douala (Bali), a large church of several hundred members. He also supervised other churches in the city. He was assisted by a lay member named Dibombé. Dibombé was a carpenter by trade and had set up a church in his workshop on the other side of Douala, not far from the bridge over the Wouri River. He regularly held public lectures there. Shortly after I left Douala, I learned of his sudden death. I am sure I will find him later with our Savior whom he loved and served so much. The memories of our stay as leaders of the littoral are numerous but have

---

[5] With the exception of the one accompanied by my children, and the one in a bush taxi, which I told above.

become a little vague, for lack of having kept a diary. The various trips throughout the conference were all accompanied by their share of problems. Often absent and far from home, I now regret not having been able to spend more time with our children. A few special hours have remained in my memory as well as in my children's. They are the rare hours spent with my son Ben and my daughter Heidi in the place we called "monkey wood" (a forest not too far from Douala). I never saw monkeys there, but it was a great place to discover countless species of butterflies. A living book to discover God's work of creation in all its beauty! Ben still talks about it today.

Before ending this chapter on the stay in Douala, I cannot fail to tell how God miraculously saved my wife for a second time.

The women's choir of the church in Douala (Bali) met once a week to rehearse. Our house was right behind the church. A small lane behind the temple connected the two buildings and the sisters came regularly to see my wife, with whom a bond of friendship had quickly developed. That evening, after rehearsal, one sister stopped by the house again before going home, chatting about the children (she had seven) and everyday things. One of them accompanied her. Without them realizing it, time passed and it was soon too late for this sister who had come from afar to return home with her youngest child. Given the late hour, my wife offered to drive her in her little car to her home. Without a moment's hesitation, the sister said yes. They left in the little "mini," accompanied by our little girl Heidi. The "mini" was, as we say in the common language, an "old car." We had bought it from a neighbor who had returned to the mainland, and the car was mainly used by Adelheid to go to Dr. Ekande's clinic. A few days before, I had taken it to the garage for a service and filled the tank well. So they left in the dark to drive our sister home. But after a half-hour drive there and back, my wife still hadn't returned after a good hour, and I started to worry. What had happened? Contacting her was impossible, I just had to wait patiently. She finally honked her horn to indicate that she was there and for me to open the gate for her. To tell you the truth, I was relieved to see her. I noticed that she was very excited and agitated and that there was a big dent in the back of her car. Without delay, she began to tell me what had happened to her on the way.

Not far from the house, on the way to the sister's house, there was a railroad crossing in the middle of town. Several people had already lost their lives there in broad daylight because neither the crossing gates nor the flashing lights were working. That evening, on her way to the dangerous spot, she slowed down and saw nothing but darkness. Now standing in the middle of the tracks, she saw a few meters away on her right, a big locomotive running without lights, without giving any signal to announce its arrival. She had just enough time to push the accelerator pedal all the way down. But that wasn't enough! The locomotive hit the back of her vehicle, where the tank was filled with gasoline. The vehicle was sent flying and landed on its four wheels, fortunately on the public highway. Being shocked by the event, she did not stop but continued on her way. When they arrived at the sister's house, they took a look at the damage without noticing any major anomalies. Adelheid and our daughter stopped for half an hour to recover a little from their emotions. Of course, there was no mobile phone to inform me. My wife gathered all her courage to return home. On arrival, I saw the damage. A nice bump on the back and two miracles to note: the axle at the back had remained in place and, even more incredible, the fuel tank had not exploded! Imagine, four people saved from certain death! "Yes Lord, You are Great." "I am with you and will rescue you, declares the LORD" (Jer. 1:8, NIV) and David describes, "Thou hast beset me behind and before, and laid thine hand upon me" (Ps. 139:5). Thank God for leaving me my dear wife!

As I recount this event, another one comes to mind. A few days later, we received a visit from Dr. Stoeger at our home in Douala. Still in total shock, my wife told Dr. Stoeger what had happened. Our host then told her in turn what he had experienced in Angola a few months earlier. There are two things to remember in order to understand what follows: Brother Stoeger was in charge of the health department of the division in Bern. Not only did he regularly travel to Cameroon to visit hospitals and dispensaries, but his presence was also needed in Angola and Mozambique, countries that were part of our division at that time. These two countries were in the middle of a civil war at the time. Thus Brother Stoeger was once called upon to go to our Bongo hospital in Huambo (Angola) which was located in the middle of rebel territory led by Savimbi. The only way to get there in an almost safe way was by plane. All land routes were risky because of mines and surprise attacks that were always possible. The plane he boarded, an old aircraft, was filled with people and luggage of all kinds. No sooner had the plane taken off than it was attacked by a ground-to-air missile. The worst part was that the missile hit one of the engines head-on. The plane shook and vibrated. Screams went up from everywhere. Flour bags came loose from the baggage compartment and even chickens started flying into the cabin (you'd be amazed at what the locals carry as hand luggage). The plane started to fall. "And I," said Brother Stoeger, "don't know why or how, but I took off my glasses in peace and quiet and said my last prayer. But oh miracle of miracles, as a former fighter pilot myself in the last war, I realized that the pilot was doing wonders to keep his plane balanced to return to the airport. He succeeded but once on the runway, he could not brake anymore. The plane continued on its crazy course and finally crashed into a wall and while everyone was waiting for the fuel to explode, nothing like that happened. All the passengers made it out safely." That night we praised God for his compassion in these trials. "God is great–beyond our understanding" (Job 36:26). Admittedly, over the years, I may have missed some of the details, but I have passed on most of what Brother Stoeger told us here.

During the years spent in Douala, the island of Equatorial Guinea was part of the Western Mission. The island is located in front of the Cameroonian coast at a distance of 30' flight. Under a very hard dictatorship for years, the country was very difficult to access because of the political situation. I personally was never able to go there but we had several churches there with a young pastor named Ricardo. On rare occasions, he was able to come and give a report. Ricardo and our churches were subject to endless difficulties. Since we left Douala, I have not heard from him again, but since the political situation has changed in the meantime, I hope he has also found an easier and more peaceful life.

I must also pay tribute to three brothers who have always supported and accompanied me in my work in Douala. I have already mentioned them earlier in my story but I repeat. They are the brothers Mongo Jean Claude, André Makong, and Etolo Bem Daniel. The latter accompanied me most of the time in my travels. They constantly assisted me with their precious actions and advice. Three brotherly men who always had at heart the evangelization for the well-being of the church and to win souls for the Lord. Brother Mongo was in charge of our churches in Douala and Brother Makong was once assigned to Bafang, in the Bamiliké country.

Before I arrived in Douala, the union brothers had voted to start our work in Bafang by building a church there, hoping that people would come. This was a miscalculation. The church remained empty and people came only sporadically. Brother Makong was sent there to follow the evangelization efforts. His work was not easy. Especially on the Sabbath, which was not about the day itself, but about the question of rest, because the motto of the local people was simply "rest is the grave." I think we learned the lesson for the future not to build a house of God without the presence of a minimum number of members rallied to the cause to form a core.

Another part of my job in Douala was to take care of the arriving and departing missionaries. For this, I was in constant contact with the Procurator of Catholic Missions, which took care of most of the customs paperwork. I also had to regularly find spare parts or replacements for

> *Since we also had a large number of colporteur evangelists, we had to be able to get the books they needed. Not to mention the many trips into the bush. The work was very varied. I was often amazed at what I was able to do.*

the maintenance of the cars, often for the college in Nanga or for other missionaries in the bush. Since we also had a large number of colporteur evangelists, we had to be able to get the books they needed. Not to mention the many trips into the bush. The work was very varied. I was often amazed at what I was able to do. Even to the point of dismantling the generator that was used to produce electricity in the bush to show evangelistic films. During these years, by the grace of God, we were able to build two permanent churches: those in Buea and Kribi. The architectural plan was designed by Heini Walder (he was the treasurer of the union for a long time). I had also started to build in the country of the Babimbis, whether it was a church or a school building, I do not remember.

But the time had come for us to think about returning to the mainland. The children needed school and we were also a little tired after spending fifteen years in the tropics. When we told the union office in Yaoundé and the division office in Bern about our decision to return, the latter put us at the disposal of our home conference in Belgium. We soon received news of our next assignment. To use the words of the letter from the Brussels office, we would again be "parachuted in" to the Grand Duchy, to replace our colleague Frans Fiscalini who had filled the gap when we left for the second time.

23. From One Mission Field to Another

The following years were full of surprises. We found the same group, except that Brother Fiscalini, through his ardent door-to-door work and by the grace of God, was able to find a couple who were then baptized. The story is a bit special in this sense: a gentleman had found in his mailbox an invitation to attend Bible courses of "The Voice," as we called it at that time. The only problem was that the man was almost 100% deaf. His wife always had to be there to make him understand by mouth. She herself, at first, had no interest, but being forced to be present to translate for her husband, she gradually became interested and discovered Jesus, her Savior. After two years, they were both baptized.

This is how we continued the Adventist work with a dozen members, all scattered over the territory of the Grand Duchy. As for everyone who leaves or returns from the missions, the first months are those in which one suffers from a "culture shock," where one must readapt to a culture in which one is not used to living. Also, I was not dealing with a church but rather a church plant. How do you do that? I thought of starting an evangelistic campaign. It was in Esch/Alzette. Thousands of invitations were distributed by the few members we had at that time. Large posters were also put up in Esch/Alzette. On the first evening, apart from a few members (only those who understood French), maybe four or five people were present, among them a Jesuit. I visited him afterwards, but without much success. However, another person present was very surprised that I came to visit her at the end. She was baptized after two years and to this day she is still part of the church. A few months later, she brought two other people, who were also baptized. What a multiplication!

I quickly understood two things and have always applied them both in Europe and in Africa. The rules are the same everywhere for successful church planting. He who does nothing can receive nothing and secondly, never neglect to visit the people contacted by conferences or "The Voice of Hope"!

> *The years have passed. They were not always been years of joy. Ups and downs were often the order of the day. But it must be said that despite their small numbers, the members never left me alone.*

The years have passed. They were not always been years of joy. Ups and downs were often the order of the day. But it must be said that despite their small numbers, the members never left me alone. During multiple "Five Day Plan" campaigns or directly evangelical conferences, I was always supported by faithful helpers for whom it was never too far or too late. One evening, I noticed that one of our members who was attending the presentation waited until the end to come out with me. When I asked him why, he said it was to walk me to my car because someone in the audience had indicated that they had brought an iron bar to beat me. Among the subjects I had dealt with during that week were the state of the dead, spiritualism, and the devil. The next day I went to the police station to report the threat. The next night the police sent a mobile patrol just in case. On another occasion, I had a "Five Day Plan" in Florenville, in the Belgian province of Luxembourg. While I was on my way, my wife who had stayed at home was called and told that I had better not do this Five Day Plan because if I did, I might soon be "pushing up daisies." Nothing like that happened, except that my wife was extraordinarily scared until I arrived home safe and sound! I also reported this threat to the local police

23. From One Mission Field to Another

because you never know! I also had in mind to launch something in Libramont, in Belgian Luxembourg. Soon the evangelical opposition showed up and accused me of being the thief of the sheep. I could never find a room for conferences. However, there were a few people there whom I had been able to contact through the correspondence courses. But at a certain point, after many studies with a family, the door was closed to me rather abruptly. I felt so discouraged that while driving through the forest of the Ardennes, I stopped on a small path in the woods and began to cry. I read Psalm 73 to encourage me:

"My foot was about to bend ... the difficulty was great in my eyes, until I entered the sanctuaries of God ... What other have I in heaven than you?" These moments of spiritual recollection did me good. There is no worse thing than discouragement when you feel abandoned and that nothing works. The only thing to do in this case is to open His Word and seek help from above, from Him who never sleeps! At some point after this incident, the devil got on my nerves. It would be better to look for work elsewhere. I would feel better than doing this thankless job. I didn't tell my family, but secretly I scoured the job ads in the newspaper. My eye was drawn to a large advertisement for a transportation company that I had worked with in Douala to clear customs and organize the transportation of our missionaries' belongings. I made an appointment with them and was soon invited to meet with the director. I was well received and we had a good and frank conversation. He said the following to me at the end of my speech and I have never forgotten it. I quote:

To this day I am grateful to have found this man in my path in the face of the devil's attack—discouragement. I think God placed him in my path to prevent me from giving up!

"Mr. Pastor, you can start with us tomorrow, but I ask you to go home and reflect on your apostolate." We shook hands and I left. As I thought about it, I realized that this man of the world had spoken to me from God. The next day I phoned him to thank him and told him that I would not be coming but would continue my pastoral ministry. To this day I am grateful to have found this man in my path in the face of the devil's attack—discouragement. I think God placed him in my path to prevent me from giving up!

But there were also remarkable facts. Let me tell you about some of them! After a "Five Day Plan," as usual, people who wanted to know a little more about our church were visited. It was not always fruitful work. A complete brochure about Adventists was handed out. I had learned this strategy from Brother R. Lenoir. Once, I had an address that showed only the telephone number and the postal code. How could I find the person indicated? I didn't call because you always run the risk of being told that they are fine and don't need further care. So I went on the hunt by asking around in the village and the search was successful. And it really was: the person was baptized two years later and is a faithful member to this day. At another time, we had distributed thousands of cards in a village, this time in Belgian Luxembourg. Months later, I received a book from the offices of "The Voice" with a request to take it to the person indicated. I noticed that the address was in the corner where we had distributed Bible study cards. In short, the woman was baptized and later her two children, one of whom is now preparing for the ministry.

In the same way, I received an address from The Voice to again take a book as a small gift to someone who had finished school. It was in a village lost between the meadows and the Ardennes Forest. A small village with a Roman church in the middle. The address I had been given was the church with the parish church next door. What was waiting for me there? A very handicapped priest opened the door for me. After I explained the reason for my visit, he invited me to come in and sit with him in the living room. Soon we were not in a discussion about who is right but rather engaged in a friendly conversation where, in the end, he assured me that the Adventist church I represented was not a cult but the church that carries the truth for our time. How glad he was to have taken the correspondence course and to have met me! We met regularly. One day I brought him

Bacchiocchi's book *From Sabbath to Sunday*. The next week he had read it completely. When, a few months later, he received a visit from Monsignor Leonard of Namur, he gave him the book and insisted that he read it and draw his conclusion. Leonard never came back to see him and the book was never returned to him. This priest advertised in his parish encouraging people to take The Voice course, but he himself was discouraged by the lack of interest in his parish. He then asked me to come and preach in his church on a Sabbath afternoon of my choice. I did so, in the middle of winter, the church was heated and many of his parishioners were present. But again, no interest in going further. I can still see him crying one day in front of me, an old man lost, not knowing what to do. He was even ready to be baptized and to join us, but only God knows why this did not happen. When he retired, he had to leave the house and I lost all trace of him.

The days and years were mostly filled with door-to-door work. Two brothers, colleagues, traveled hundreds of kilometers to give me a hand. One was Léon Liénard and the other Léon Pollin; the latter was in charge of peddling. Both of them were astonished at the lack of receptivity of the population, they wished me a lot of courage and "God with you." As I was alone from the beginning, I continued like that. One has experiences with people and also with one's God who always opened enough doors for me in summer to be sheltered and to be warm during the harsh winters.

For some time, our little church needed a fixed place. We would soon have to leave the place lent to us for years by the community, which needed it. We had already been looking for a long time for a place to build a church house. Now it was time to act without hesitation. We found a piece of land. The money was still lacking. We visited the members and soon we had the necessary capital to start. Brother E. Lüdescher (then president of the division) promised us the following help: every franc from our pocket was an additional franc from the division. An offer not to be ignored or missed. We were soon able to buy the land and the construction work began, with each member adding his or her share of manual labor. We invested every moment of our free time in the construction. Whole families were present every Sunday. The building grew in an amazing way and

The pulpit of the church of Mersch

was finally inaugurated on May 11, 1985. Apart from our brothers responsible for all levels of our organization, the Mayor of Mersch and the parish priest responsible for the local Roman church also came to the inauguration party. This was followed by a series of well-attended lectures. A few months later, I again launched "Five Day Plans" to help smokers quit. A gentleman who attended became interested in the gospel and asked me to visit him. We soon had him visit us on Sabbath morning for worship. That same day, our church elder put out a call for a volunteer to build a new pulpit according to the plan he had in hand.

The visiting gentleman came, after the church service, to offer himself for this work. A few months later, the masterpiece was delivered and has been adorning the worship hall ever since.

This work will not be enough to tell the story of all the other events that took place. One thing is certain: time flies! In the meantime, our children have grown up and soon left home to follow their own path, the normal course of life...

24. Central African Republic (CAR)

We received a letter from Berne, from Brother Steveny, secretary of the Adventist Work for Europe and West Africa. The work in the CAR needs a missionary in view of Hans Obenaus' move to Chad to help with construction in Béré. Brother Steveny, at that time secretary of the division, asks us if we do not want to take up the "pilgrim's staff" again to go back to Africa, this time to CAR (Central African Republic), where an experienced missionary and a nurse were needed to set up a health post at the Bangui station, in the Castor neighborhood where the CAR mission headquarters was located. The children having already left home, our decision to respond favorably was not long in coming. However, one condition had to be fulfilled before leaving: finding a replacement to continue the work in Luxembourg. This was not easy. A candidate who speaks the two main languages of the country, French and German, was needed. After several months of searching, they found Brother Gérard Fridlin, a pastor in France. In January 1990, we left for Bangui. To get to this landlocked country in the middle of Africa, we took a plane. Hans met us at the airport. Once outside the airfield, we were suddenly hit by culture shock. After years spent in Europe with all its abundance, beautiful houses, supermarkets filled even with so many things you don't need, its almost perfect infrastructure, we landed again in one of the poorest countries on earth. The day was already on its way out. It was dark when we left the airport. Apart from a little street lighting, the darkness was only pierced by storm lights in front of a store here and there. There were a lot of people on foot, and the roads were full of potholes. What world was waiting for us here?

Before leaving Europe, we had made the necessary purchases to set up the health station. We had shipped a 1 cubic meter crate of materials and medicines to start the medical work. We were still waiting for it. ADRA of the new African Division with its headquarters in Abidjan, was represented by David Syme. He came a few weeks later to welcome us and encourage us to launch ADRA in the Central African Republic in its various aspects. We would soon have the necessary finances to move forward with the health post. At least, that is what he promised us. In the meantime, my wife had to help me with the office paperwork and the printing of the sabbath school quarterlies on the old stencil machine. These lessons translated into Sango had to be typed on the stencils, after which we had to put them one by one on the machine and add ink regularly to print the booklets for the coming quarter. Whole evenings were invested in this. At the end of each session, it seemed that more ink had been used to black ourselves than to print our lessons. We must not forget that this work was often done by the poor light of a kerosene lamp. Another brother (whose name I have forgotten) was in charge of the translation of this sabbath school quarterlies as well as the correction of the "Voice of Hope" lessons.

It was dark when we left the airport. Apart from a little street lighting, the darkness was only pierced by storm lights in front of a store here and there. There were a lot of people on foot, and the roads were full of potholes. What world was waiting for us here?

Let's go back to our arrival in January 1990. Hans had one month to introduce me to the territory and to show me the many churches that had already been planted for a few years and that were scattered throughout

24. Central African Republic (CAR)

the country, this enormous territory of 1000 kilometers by 500. Since the arrival of Jean Kempf and his family in 1960, the image of the Adventist church had already changed. I can only recommend reading his book *Va! Je Suis Avec Toi!* to get an idea of the pioneering work he did. When we arrived 30 years later, several missionaries had already followed the Kempfs, among them the Sanguessa, Otchofsky, Giger, and Obenaus families. And there are probably still a few missing whose names I have forgotten in my list. Not that they are of lesser importance, but my memory fails me. They are the ones who built churches like those in Zima, Alindao, Bambari, Bria, Bangassou, and others.

I admire these families who were ready to move far from civilization. They were often without news of their relatives or friends for months. To get to Bangui, they had to venture almost a whole day on dusty or muddy tracks to travel a few hundred kilometers. The result of these years of devotion and sacrifice culminated in an SDA church already well established with 2,500 members at the time we arrived. It was now up to us to plant ADRA and continue the evangelism.

One of the first trips with Hans was to Sibut, a town located 200 kilometers from Bangui. It was one of the only paved roads, but again we had to be careful of potholes. A former pastoral worker had lived there, who had to be fired for reasons I don't want to mention here. This is not my purpose either. The reason for our trip to Sibut was to visit the daughter of our former pastor who was possessed by an evil spirit. We found her bedridden. Her father was absent. Only her mother was present. We were able to talk to her.

We then approached her daughter and knelt before her. We prayed that the Lord would deliver the young woman but every time the name "Jesus" was mentioned in the prayer, a loud screaming sound was heard. The girl was not delivered from the demon that possessed her. We left the place and left the poor girl under God's grace. Not everyone has the gift of deliverance. Or was it the wickedness of the ex-pastor that came into play here? Only God knows and that is enough for us.

25. On the Way to Ouadda

Before he left, Hans insisted that we go to visit the few new members far away in the Upper Kotto. I think it was in Ouadda, not far from the Sudanese border. In Hans' Mercedes, which became mine after he left for Chad, we left for several days. Just a few days before our departure, some of our belongings arrived by freight. In this cargo was a tent to be installed on the roof of the car. Great for Africa: we slept high, dry, and out of danger from wild animals. With the folding tent on the roof, Adelheid was

On the way to Ouadda

25. On the Way to Ouadda

tempted to accompany us, which she did. On the first day, we traveled the 450 kilometers from Bangui to Bria. The next day, very early in the morning, after asking God to accompany us, we crossed the river Boungou by ferry. We wanted to take the shortest route, the one Hans still wanted to discover before leaving for Chad. We soon realized that it was not a road but worse than a bush track. Not far from where we crossed the Boungou on the ferry, a truck was blocking the way.

This fully loaded vehicle was stuck in the fine sand, never to get out again, I thought. With great difficulty, in four-wheel drive plus the differential, we passed this sandy place. We then entered unknown territory. A track completely invaded by wild grass and other tropical plants, to the point where we were about to turn back. Only, for some reason that I have forgotten, they had removed the protective plate from the front radiator. So, if a branch or something else was going to pierce the radiator, we could only rely on the grace of God. We moved slowly forward without ever encountering a village or a human being. What an adventure we were

Open-pit gold mine

on! After a hundred kilometers, we finally heard the sound of engines, water pumps, and people. We had arrived at an open-pit diamond and gold mine where everyone was working independently.

Happy to find a living soul, we stopped for a few moments but, considering the advanced time and the journey still to accomplish, we left without delay. The night falls quickly in these countries and it was soon dark. Without a road map (but what good is a map when there is only one way to go?), we were looking at the stars that shine very clearly in the African nights when the road suddenly stopped in front of another river, the Kotto. It was around 8 pm. Seeing a fire on the other side, we called, yes, we shouted, to the boatman, hoping that he would hear us and be willing to take us so late. This man must have taken pity on us because he actually came to pick us up. When we arrived on the other side of the river, the man invited us to spend the night in his village, next to his own hut. The way to Ouadda was still long and dangerous at night. That evening, we were invited to spend the evening around a nice fire to talk.

The man was happy to have strangers in his home, a rarity in these remote areas, and we were happy to have found someone who assured us that this trail indeed led to Ouadda. Listening to the night sounds of the bush and looking up to the sky, we talked about the wonders of God's creation, the Fall and the wonderful Plan of Salvation. The third day of the journey, which seemed endless and full of the unknown, passed without any other spectacular incidents. The road was now more passable and late in the afternoon we arrived at our destination. The news of our arrival spread as quickly as a bushfire. We gathered with our members and of course many visitors. I never thought I would find members of the Adventist Church in this place. Never had a pastor or missionary set foot here, but if I remember correctly, it was a church member who had been posted there for his work. Then, as the people here say, everything worked "by street radio," God has his sheep everywhere and he knows how to find them! When evening came, we got ready for the night. We set up our folding tent on the roof of the Mercedes and Hans made his bed under the stars, between our brother's house and the car we were going to ride in.

25. On the Way to Ouadda

But this night was to be remembered for the rest of our lives. While we were sleeping, Adelheid opened her eyes and then woke me up. "Can't you feel anything? The car keeps moving. You have to go and see what's going on. Indeed I also noticed movements, as if someone was rubbing against the vehicle. Having seen a lot of goats and sheep in the evening before going to bed, I answered: "No, it's nothing serious! It's just the sheep rubbing against the sides of the car. If it was anything else, Hans would probably wake up. At least, that's what he said, "I wake up with the slightest noise and I'll sleep next to the car. So rest easy!" The movements stopped a little later and we went back to sleep. But, oh, what a surprise when we woke up! Hans was still sleeping peacefully next to the car, but it was empty! A thief had come in the night, removed the car windows and emptied the car of its contents without difficulty. They were not sheep or goats and Hans was not as good a guard as he wanted us to believe! After reporting to the local police (which took all morning) followed by a short pirogue trip on the Pipi river, where we saw hippos, which allowed us to relax for a few moments

But, oh, what a surprise when we woke up! Hans was still sleeping peacefully next to the car, but it was empty! A thief had come in the night, removed the car windows and emptied the car of its contents without difficulty.

from all the stress we had experienced in the last few days, we took the direct road to Bria this time, which was not much better than the one we had taken before. From Bria, we drove down to Bambari to head to Bangassou, where Hans still wanted to finish the roof of our local pastor's house and show me the Zima station not far from Bangassou. When, after a week, we were back in Bangui, we had traveled some 2000 kilometers. It was an overview of a part of the territory where we were going to work. We would have to discover the western part of the country on our own, as it was time for Hans to leave with his family. The trip would have to be made at night because of the danger of the road bandits. Traveling at night was indeed safer, since the army, in order to protect the movement of civilian cars, also made trips at night. Thus, the road bandits were wary of attacks because they did not know whether it was a military or civilian car that was coming. Before leaving that evening, we had another prayer meeting to beg the Lord to grant His mercy and protection to the Obenaus family on their way to their new field of work in Chad. Their first station was Béré, in order to work one the hospital building; then N'Djamena, then Ngaoundéré in Cameroon. We, on the other hand, were now left to the grace of God. The culture shock was slowly giving way to the reality of daily life. In the evenings, the electricity was cut off from 7:00 p.m. until 10:00 p.m. or later to save the diesel needed to run the turbines that produced the city's power. We often had no water, I don't know why but they always found a reason to justify the cut off. Now I had to start driving in a city where, at every corner, there was a policeman (or a policewoman) who, at any time of the day, could stop you to check the papers of your car and your identity. You get used to it quite quickly, except for my wife who quickly gave up driving because of the endless harassments of this kind. However, we had to visit our stations in the west of the country, Bouar, Berberati, not to mention the church in Beloko, a village on the border with Cameroon. We spent weeks on the road to visit these places where workers or lay members had settled. They were often remote and isolated from the civilized world as we know it in our home countries. When I mention the village of Beloko, it is not without reason. This is the story of our church in this remote area 500 kilometers from Bangui.

26. You're Going to Worship the Beast?

Youssouf was a member of the church in Bangui. He was a police inspector in the Bangui region, a good Christian and a convinced Roman Catholic. He never failed to go to mass every Sunday. So, one Sunday morning, on his way to church, he was greeted by one of his neighbors (a member of the Bangui Adventist Church) who, like most Africans, spends a lot of time at the front door. That morning, seeing his neighbor going to church, our brother greeted him and asked, "Youssouf, where are you going now?" "To church, of course!" replied Youssouf, to which our brother promptly replied, "Oh, you're going to worship the beast?" That doesn't seem like the best introduction to doing evangelism. Yet Youssouf turned around and asked him what he meant by that. The conversation began or, better yet, the Bible study began. Our brother Youssouf himself told me about this encounter. After two hours of conversation with many questions and answers, Youssouf went home without going to his church. He went to tell his wife what he had discovered that morning. Not only the real church but "Jesus." He was baptized soon after. As a police inspector, he was often assigned to places where no one had ever heard of Adventists. So, he could think of nothing better than to begin evangelizing the people around his new assignment and eventually built a small church (by his own means) for the new members to meet on Sabbath.

The church in Beloko on the border with Cameroon

One night I was able to talk to this group of people who were meeting in the village where Youssouf was a representative of the law and government and at the same time a missionary of the Adventist Church. In these circumstances, Youssouf, by the grace of God, brought forth many groups and small churches.

27. We Want to See…

One of our members (was he a schoolmaster? I don't remember the details) had gone to settle in a place that had not yet been reached by our message. The name of the village escapes me, but Adelheid, who accompanied me during those days, kept a kind of detailed diary which we have just found by chance as I write these lines. Here is in a few words her description of this trip. We had to go to Paoua in the province of Ouham Pende, near the border with Chad, about 500 kilometers from Bangui. The good brother in question had started to spread the Word. The only thing that stood in the way was that the villagers, having never heard of Adventists, were asking the questions: "What kind of church is this? And aren't you a false prophet? Your message is good, but how do we know that you are not false? Bring us the missionary who represents this church. We want to see him. Then we will believe you." When the brother came to Bangui to tell me about his problem and his efforts to get our message across, I was really surprised. In the days of Africanization, was the missionary still given such importance? On the other hand, I was pleased to see that the time of the missionaries was not yet over. The village was located in a place completely unknown to us. Only, the roads were becoming less and less safe at that time, because of the road bandits, as I mentioned earlier.

It had already happened to me once, on the way to Sibut, to suddenly find a pile of pieces of trees blocking the road. It was impossible to pass: first we had to get out of the vehicle to remove the obstacle, and some young people took advantage of this to burst forth, machetes in hand. They wanted to help us to open the passage, "but please sir…" We understood very quickly the miserable situation of these young people. I was able to talk to them a little and a few bills, given out of pity, did the trick so that they would clear the wood that was in the way. This incident showed the degradation of security in the country. Regularly and more and more often, the noises of the road bandits intensified. They were even often violent, and from time to time, the aggression ended in murder. News reached us from another Protestant mission station that one of their pastors had been killed in such an ambush.

We had already postponed the trip to Paoua several times, but our brother insisted more and more that we come, despite the growing insecurity. If we waited, travel would certainly become even more dangerous. Adelheid dates this trip to August 1990. After driving 350 kilometers, we arrived in Bossangoa. It was a Friday afternoon. She mentions in her diary that Bossangoa is only a large village with an elementary school, a high school, a maternity ward, and a dispensary where all the medicines were missing. There was no electricity or running water and the villagers' fields were 12 kilometers from their homes. The members, like the other villagers, spent the whole week in their fields, given the distance. On Friday afternoons, they returned to spend the Sabbath with their families and other members. The church was the result of a pioneer's work. A pastor (whose name I have forgotten) had started an evangelistic work here in 1985. He bought a piece of land, made clay bricks, and built his house and a chapel. A volunteer brother from Europe finally came to help him finish the work. I never knew his name.

The Friday night, Sabbath morning, Sabbath afternoon, and evening meetings were well-attended. All the members as well as visitors gathered in large numbers. It seemed that there was no end to the preaching, one meeting after another: the people wanted to learn. We drove to Paoua on Sunday morning. Another 150 kilometers and the further we went towards our final destination, the worse the condition of the road became. After many tiring hours, we finally arrived where they wanted to see the missionary! Adelheid wrote in her diary: "... another town but smaller than the previous one, no drinking water, no health care, no electricity, nothing like that here. But on the other hand, a lot of poverty and disease. There are so many things missing here. And yet, we found an Adventist church here as a result of the work of a brother who one day decided to move here to proclaim the love of Christ in this lost place. About sixty people attended the meetings and we still had to make several pastoral home visits. We were invited to have the evening meal at the home of the village midwife. The hospitality of the people is indescribable and everyone could take it as an example," Adelheid remarked in her story. Until late at night, we talked to each other and exchanged experiences. We spoke of God's love and the wonders of his creation, without neglecting suffering with its many questions. We parted very late to go to bed but not without thanking God for this meeting and asking for His blessing for the night. We settled down in our apartment on the roof of the car. Soon after, it started to rain. From 3 am to 9 am, a torrential downpour tested the waterproofing of our tent on wheels. The next morning, it was time to start the return trip. The problem was that, after these hours of deluge, the rain barriers, installed every 30 kilometers, would be closed and, usually, no car is allowed to pass for 6 to 8 hours, time necessary to dry the roads a little and avoid more serious damages because of traffic. When you are in front of a barrier and it rains again in the meantime, six more hours are added. So, if you are unlucky, the way back can take days. Fortunately, before leaving Bangui, I had obtained a ministerial authorization that gave me priority to pass, even after heavy rains. These rain barriers, as I said, are present every 30 kilometers. With our authorization, we had no problem waiting, but what opportunities to talk with the people in charge of the checkpoints and to distribute brochures and even books! Many copies of *Steps to Christ* found their way into places where Jesus was not yet known. On several occasions, the guards at the rain gates were astonished that we had obtained this exceptional permission, which is normally only reserved for ministers or, exceptionally, for direct government employees. How I obtained this permit is another story that you can read in the next chapter.

28. What Does He Want from Me?

We had two or three evangelical peddlers. They tried to earn their living by selling evangelical and health literature. In a country where the percentage of literacy is still developing and money is often very scarce, it is not always easy to find readers who have money and are willing to spend it on a book. However, he who seeks finds! Some of our peddlers often went around the cities of the country in the hope of finding some buyers. For example, one of these brave brothers (whose name I have forgotten) once went to Alindao, in the Lower Kotto. That day, the Minister of Finance of the Central African Republic, Mr. Wazoua Dieudonné, was visiting Alindao for an administrative meeting with the chiefs and officials of the small town. From a distance, our brother was following the meeting and was constantly gesturing, as if he wanted to approach the high dignitary. The latter noticed his efforts and ordered one of his bodyguards to go and ask what this person wanted from him. "An interview with the Minister" was his answer. And miraculously, this interview was granted. Happily, our brother said who he was and showed all his literature. Indeed, the government representative was not only interested in the books, of which he bought several copies, but also in the Adventist faith that our brother was talking about. His interest became so intense that Bible studies were regularly held. This is what the former minister told me personally.

I was unaware of all this, until one day our peddler brother came into my office with a big smile and told me that Mr. Minister of Finance was ready for baptism. When could we organize it? I didn't immediately understand what he was trying to tell me or whether he was telling me a joke or something else. However, he insisted and I was soon convinced of the seriousness of his words. Still, I found it a little abnormal that the president of the conference was not aware of such an event. The next day, I went to the ministry in question to ask for a meeting with the Minister, who received me without keeping me waiting. We had a cordial meeting. He was as happy to meet me as I was to meet him. To be sure that he was really ready for baptism, I invited him to attend the services on Sabbath mornings and to come to our house for further studies.

The next Sabbath he came to church in his ministerial car with his bodyguard and on Sunday morning he arrived at our house, again in his ministerial car, accompanied by his bodyguard. As his position required, he was often touring the country but when he was there, his presence was

Baptism of the Minister of Finance of the CAR

certain. At one point, he told me that he had spoken to the President of the Republic and that from now on, he should not rely on him for government business because the Sabbath is the Lord's day. The president was astonished and asked for an explanation. This had been the occasion to give a study on the Sabbath, with the advice that he too, as President of the Republic, had better keep that day. It seems that from that moment on, the President of CAR no longer held meetings and did not go to his farm on Saturdays. A few months later, the brother minister was baptized. I gave the privilege to the elder of the church in Bangui, Tita, to baptize his minister. The new brother had organized a great feast for this Sabbath where all the members and other guests enjoyed themselves. It was an unforgettable Sabbath! For the rest of our time in the CAR, this brother was a faithful member of the church in Bangui. After we left, I often wondered what had become of this brother. Until two years ago when, by a stroke of luck, I learned from a church member in France (Pierre Kempf) that this brother was faithfully attending the church that he himself was attending. A few weeks later, I took the train to see him. What a joy to meet my brother, the one I used to visit at his ministerial office so many years ago! He is now a faithful and diligent member of the Adventist church in the city where he lives. Accompanying him on my arrival at the station were Brother Jean Kempf and his wife, the two pioneers of our work in the Central African Republic, who started there in the 1960s. It was during this meeting that the former minister gave me some details about how his contact with the church came about[6]. Yes, "God is great"! Are we willing to see and acknowledge Him?

---

[6]The Minister (Wazoua Dieudonné) was interrogated by Sylvie Loïal, who wrote a book about his life and how he became an Adventist. I'm also mentioned in the book. After a "coup" Wazoua fled the country with the precious help of the members of the SDA Banqui church and is living now in peace in France. The book is called "De lautre côté du fleuve" by Sylvie Loïal and edited by éditions PALANGEE. My story is completely independent of this book. I got details from Wazoua when I did visit him in France.

29. Our Father ... You Know the Rest

One evening, one of the elders from the church in Bangui came to visit me. We sat on the terrace of the house. It was one of those evenings that you can only enjoy in the tropics. The sun already down, a full moon, and a little breeze that cools you down from the sweat that beads on your body and you still hear the sounds of the crickets around you, one of those African evenings that you can't forget. But there is something else that I can't forget about this encounter. The incredible story of my brother and friend Tita Samba Sole who was visiting me and is still an elder in the Adventist church in Bangui. He began to tell me what had happened to him some twenty years earlier. "Do you know that you have before you a man condemned to death?" "How could I know?" was my answer.

"Tell me!" And he began to tell me his story. I tried, 25 years later, to remember the details of his story and put it on paper. I was afraid of making mistakes, so I tried to contact him and ask him to verify. I am passing on the story as he corrected it for me. However, it is as if I were telling it. He probably wanted to keep my style. It's a little long, but I think it's worth passing on in its entirety.

When Bokassa took power, several attempted coups followed a few years later. But that of the twin brothers Obrou and Meya, perpetrated on February 3, 1976, where Bokassa had been saved in extremis by a miracle coup, this crisis gave Bokassa the opportunity to review his bodyguard. It should be remembered that during this attempt, the perpetrators threw grenades while

Bokassa was reviewing the troops who had come to the airport for the honors during a trip to the interior of the country. It should be noted that the perpetrators of the overthrow were all convicted and killed.

Tita-Samba Solé was hired as one of his bodyguards. Wherever Bokassa went, Tita accompanied him. Thus, he saw almost all the countries of the world, even China, with the all-powerful Jean Bedel Bokassa (well, Bokassa thought he was all-powerful!).

After having attended a training course in Egypt for the protection of high personalities, Bokassa, who was visiting this part of Africa, obliged the young Tita to shorten his training in order to come back to consolidate his protection because coup attempts were recurrent at that time.

Back home, some officers in the Central African bureaucracy, jealous of the few favors Tita enjoyed from Bokassa, invented a big lie about him. Nothing better than to accuse him of being in the pay of the Egyptian president of the time, Anouar EL SADATE, in order to overthrow him, and then again by spreading the rumor that he was making sweet eyes at the one affectionately called "The Romanian," one of Bokassa's wives. For this affair, Tita was arrested with four other soldiers and a nurse, the nursemaid of his last-born child with the Romanian woman. Without a trial, the fate of Tita and his companions in misery was sealed: "condemned to death."

Tita-Samba, born into a Catholic family, never knew how to pray from what he told me. In Béréngo (the name of Bokassa's palace), late at night, a few men in uniform came to the place where the five soldiers had been put because the only woman in the group had been deported to a police station in Pissa, a small town a few kilometers from Béréngo.

Given the special nature of his accusation, Tita was the first to be taken out, handcuffed and shackled, and led into the darkness where a firing squad was waiting. According to Tita, it was at this moment that he understood that he was going to be executed. He began to pray to God in these words:

"Our Father who art in heaven, hallowed be thy name, thy will be done on earth as it is in heaven... You Know the Rest."

"You know the rest" is a clear demonstration that even the universal prayer was not known to Tita-Samba. He instinctively repeated this prayer. It is later that one will say to him that the platoon had difficulties distinguishing him well in the dark night. Instructions were thus given to cover him with a white bag, which was done. Had it not been for the intervention of Georges, Bokassa's eldest son, he would have been shot that evening of October 6, 1977, three days after his arrest.

The young men (average age 23 years), were deported on the orders of the great Chief to the prison of Ngaragba. It was in this house of incarceration that the abuse of the soldiers-prisoners of Bokassa really began. The jailers took care to separate the group in two, after a systematic search. Alone, Tita was taken to a cell called "Safari," the name of a hotel in the capital. He remained there six days without being fed. During this time, his other colleagues were taken to the "Red Door," a cell reserved exclusively for political prisoners.

Late in the night of October 13, the captain, jailer of the prison, arrived with his agents for the dirty work. God was still with Tita-Samba. This time, he was taken out of the cell, handcuffed, crossed in the back, and pushed forward. Behind him, two torturers each hold the end of the chain. When they are about to put the chain around his neck, a miracle happens: the telephone rings. The sentry who was on duty ran to the firing squad to tell the captain-general: "Papa is on the line," to say that it was Bokassa himself who was on the phone.

After a quick conversation, the captain went back to order a different prisoner to be taken out because there was a "mistake made." The young Tita-Samba still had his life saved.

On New Year's Eve, while behind the big fence of the prison, one could listen to the songs of joy of the neighboring population, they shouted "Happy New Year" but these populations were almost unaware of what was happening inside this prison, this old building from the colonial era.

Tita's companions were taken out one by one, supposedly to be heard either in court or at the Council of Ministers. This is the version that the extracted prisoners were made to believe. In reality, they were immediately killed on Bokassa's instructions or, in some cases, as a result of settling accounts.

More than two months later, the scenario of the execution of children, pupils, and students has taken center stage in the macabre news of this prison. You will recall that the fate of Bokassa had been sealed in Kigali following the popular uprising, especially the children who were arrested and tortured to death in Ngaragba prison.

Food was too often in short supply. On the rare occasions that food entered the prison, it was always plantains, taro, cassava leaves, and sometimes meat or fish. And when there was no food to survive (I can still hear him telling me this), he would put pieces of bananas on the corrugated iron sheets of the roof so that they would dry out and he could feed himself with these provisions.

The routine life in Ngaragba's prison of death forced Tita and his elders (since he was in "solitary confinement," a compartment for those sentenced to death along with those who had spent ten years in prison) to devote themselves to prayer.

In solitary confinement, there were a dozen prisoners. From the simple witch doctor to army officers and non-commissioned officers and diplomats—all of them were waiting for death to come. That is, if Bokassa decided it would or if there was an unfortunate incident in the solitary confinement yard.

Tita does not forget the case that cost the life of the young veterinarian Antoine. The latter had been arrested for having been clumsy when he was taken to treat the monarch's flock of sheep. Two or three animals had not survived the medicines administered. For these reasons, Antoine was directly thrown into isolation, without any trial. One afternoon, when it was his turn to stand guard, he saw his cousin Joseph through the crack in the door of his cell. He began to call out. Surprised by a soldier who was right next door, Antoine was joined that same evening by his cousin in solitary confinement. To make matters worse, they were executed for this imprudence, as it was not allowed for the prisoners to have contact with the outside world.

There were other cases such as that of cousins Antoine and Joseph who marked the three long and painful years of Tita, spent under the reign of Bokassa.

There is also nature–I mean the environment–and the dreams that marked the lives of Bokassa's prisoners. Our friend Tita-Samba tells us that they often observed the crows flying over their heads. Their cawing edified them. The rats that lived with them in this sinister place were the object of their observation. Sometimes, some unusual signs made them believe that something was happening.

Tita and his companions in misery could only live in their dreams. One night, Tita had a dream in which he was told that he would be freed. In this dream, he was to go to the place where he had first played handball. He would find a church in that place. He and his companions would ask its pastor to be baptized. The first Adventist station was actually built there by the Kempf couple.

A few more weeks (or months) passed and Bokassa was overthrown. Afterwards, all the political prisoners are released and with them our friend Tita. He was taken away in a military car and asked where to go.

Not knowing where to go, he described to the military the place that had been indicated to him in his dream. One of the soldiers understood. He took him to the Adventist Mission in the Castors district. When he saw the place, he recognized it. The four friends, now former prisoners, went to the Adventist church in Bangui. They stayed there for 3 days and 3 nights in fasting and prayer. They asked Pastor Clément Colongondat to baptize them on September 25, 1979. Tita resumed his studies in communication. He became a famous journalist and remained a faithful member of the church in the CAR. During my years in the CAR, he was an elder of the church and he was, during this time, a precious help in difficult and often painful moments. In 1990, he was sent to the General Conference in Indianapolis as a delegate from the CAR and we met in San Antonio at the General Conference in 2015.

Here is what he told me: "My childhood was marked by the lack of fatherly love and I quickly opted for my own defense. I started with boxing, judo and karate; all violent sports to defend myself! Then, at the age of 18, I had my eldest daughter without God. I started making music with friends who were obsessed with drinking and smoking joints.

There was often verbal and physical abuse. Then I opened the door to active life. I was recruited by the police and then assigned to the guard of the President of the Republic. I kept bad company and became uncontrollable. Discouraged by my life, I tried to commit suicide in a car accident. After all this, God guided me to another city without my knowing it, to prison where I didn't know anyone and I started again from scratch.

Brother Tita, as a delegate, whom I met again at the GC in Sant Antonio in 2015

I met friends, the youngest of whom had already spent six years in prison and the oldest of whom had nine years of incarceration under their belt. They brought me to God through long nights of prayer and devotions and there I accepted Jesus into my life! I became, by the grace of God, the witness who witnessed all the executions of my colleagues and other prisoners who came after me. Another great miracle: the new birth.

I was thirsty for the Word and its teachings. After praying, I made a promise to God. If I came out of that prison alive, I would serve him until death. What a deliverance! What a relief! I found peace and freedom: more miracles! I have become a wonderful creature thanks to Jesus. I am joyful and happy with this new life in Jesus and I thank God for all his benefits for me and his powerful Word because without him, I am nothing and would be dead but here I live with him and I have eternally the true life!

This is the life of our brother Tita.

When he finished his story, I could not say anything but think of this word found in Romans 11:33: "O the depth of the riches both of the wisdom and knowledge of God! how unsearchable are his judgments, and his ways past finding out!" Often we pray and it seems that the prayer goes no higher than the ceiling. Yet God listens, even if he doesn't answer right away. Israel had to pray 400 years before God delivered them to the promised land. The time was probably not yet right? When I went to bed that night, I had some things to think about before I went to sleep.

30. Conferences in Bangui

Between the many trips in this country twice the size of France, we had to find a time to conduct an evangelistic campaign in Bangui itself. It was decided to hold a seminar on Daniel in our temple in the capital. However, we had some problems with publicity. There was no way to print posters, so we started to work by hand.

I spent entire evenings drawing large posters. There was a shortage of storefronts in town, but there were enough trees to stick them up! The

Bangui station with its chapel

30. Conferences in Bangui

"flyers" were printed on the mission's old stencil printer. I don't remember how many we printed but it was a lot. The church members made sure to distribute them to everyone in town. I can't forget the precious help of our brother Tita who was at that time a journalist at the national radio and had no problem announcing the conferences daily and free of charge on the airwaves of Radio Bangui. We were all waiting to know how many people were going to come for the cycle that was going to last seven days. But to our surprise, there was not enough room in the church to accommodate all the people. Many had to settle for standing room only. It seemed like the numbers were growing every night. At the end of the cycle, we held Bible studies for those who wanted to learn more about our message. Forty-five people came the following Thursday night for the Bible class. I will never forget the words of a fairly young man who at one point stood up in the audience with concern in his heart and said to me, "Pastor, you give us light and a lot of truth that I can't argue with. But you must know that I am a Catholic. I will not be baptized by you because the moment I become an Adventist, I will never be able to preach these truths in my church. I have access to it now. Being an Adventist, I wouldn't have it anymore!" By the end of that campaign, about 20 people had been baptized and as far as I know, most of them are still there. Not long ago, one of them gave me a phone call while in Paris to say hello and remind me of that wonderful week at the Daniel seminar where he had come to know the Lord so many years ago. As I write this memoir, just a week ago, I received a call. On the other end of the line, I heard, "Hello, Pastor, how are you? It's Daniel. Do you remember me, Daniel from the conferences in Bangui, Laurentine's brother? We were baptized in Bangui after the seminar on Daniel, 25 years ago." Yes, I still remember how, after their diligent presence for more than a week, I went to visit them at their home to encourage them. Two young people, with no job and no secure future, but with hearts full of joy for this wonderful news of the gospel they had found. How could I forget moments like that? I read in the bible in Psalm 126: 5: "Those who sow with tears will reap with songs of joy." What a truth!

I must open a parenthesis here. Since our arrival in 1990, we were waiting for the funds to start the installation of a health post, after the renovation of a certain classroom. We had brought with us all the necessary material, well packed in a big box of 1 cubic meter: medicines, instruments, bandages, etc. But the funds that had been promised to us were still lacking. All the letters I wrote remained unanswered. Fortunately, we also brought a dozen sewing machines to start a sewing class. Adelheid started with sewing lessons. On other days, when I was not on tour, I taught the men (young and old) about agriculture where I had some knowledge. Both classes were well attended and ADRA lived up at least in part to its reputation as a "development aid" organization. Since the health center was still not launched, Adelheid had the opportunity to accompany me on my rounds several times, when office work permitted.

One day I started a different kind of evangelistic campaign: a "Five Day Plan". In a country where young and old are still heavily misled by mass advertising for cigarettes and become slaves to tobacco, a new wind had to blow. Tita, through his contacts as a journalist, helped us to get the big hall of the capital. A few signs here and there in the city and the advertisements made by Tita on the radio, not to mention the work of the "street radio" by the members of the church, filled the hall well from the first night. This was also the case on all the following nights. But strangely enough, on the fifth night, a completely different audience began to mingle with our regular listeners. We were more and more surprised when someone started setting up I don't know what on the stage. A few of our helpers went to find out what was going on. Shortly thereafter, they came to tell me that the janitor had mistakenly rented out the room that night to two different events. Since the other gathering was much larger than ours, we were relegated to a secondary room. But the secondary room was really small. More than half of our audience had to follow this last presentation under the starry sky. In any case, our Five Day Plan was a success. Weeks later, we met people who still expressed their gratitude to us for helping them overcome the bondage of smoking.

What we find in the whole world is that no one lives forever. "There is a time for everything" wrote Solomon, "... a time to be born and a time to die" (Eccles. 3:1). In the society where I lived at that time, mourning lasts several days. Once the person is buried, the influx of visitors continues for several more days. The circle of acquaintances and friends, where everyone knows everyone else, is much larger than in our society, where it is made up only of close family members and a few friends. When it was a member of the church, I also went there to express my compassion and sympathy while saying some spiritual words for those who wanted to hear them. The next day was the funeral, which I also attended. I thought it would be a funeral like any other but one thing struck me. The closer we got to the cemetery, the more hearses entered the burial grounds. I asked my brother Tita, who was with me, how this was done. The cars were lining up to enter and there were so many people! There was a constant coming and going. To which my brother gently replied, "There are two causes of death here, Pastor, AIDS and malaria." Sad situation because the two main reasons could have been avoided. I thought again, "Dying is one thing, but what is serious is that these early deaths could have been avoided!"

31. Berberati

One of the places I went to quite often was Berberati in Mambéré-Kadei, some 500 kilometers from the capital. Each time it was a trip on "corrugated iron" roads. The main reason was the construction of the chapel. The old building was dilapidated, so Hans had started a new one. Every time I saw it, it seemed to me that with the first strong wind, the whole thing would fall down. The building made me feel ashamed. I had to find the necessary means to finish the work.

The old church at Berberati

31. Berberati

The new church at Berberati

By the grace of God, we would find them. We also had to find a serious mason to finish the work on the new church, which had been started a few years earlier. Only a few walls were built. The rest of the walls and a good roof were still missing.

A local merchant was able to provide us with the necessary materials such as cement, wood for the beams, and metal sheets. But the work had to be supervised, hence the reason for my many visits. At the same time, it was a blessing for the local church because each time I was there, we had several spiritual meetings and seeing that the new building was progressing, the members (and me too) were happy to soon have a building worthy of a church. The work was completed several months later. The time for the dedication was set. I only had one problem getting there. For some time now, I had needed a special permit to go there, because of the open diamond and gold mines in those areas. However, the problem was not the permit, but the roads made dangerous because of the road bandits. The security in the country had deteriorated further, so much so that

I looked for other ways to get there. But how? Berberati had an airport for small private planes, but who was still using it? I knocked on the doors of other missions and companies but nothing, no flight! Fortunately, I had quite good relations with the Minister of Internal Affairs of the country, probably thanks to the Minister of Finance who was now, for several months, our brother. I don't remember the details, but I went to the Minister in question to ask him to find me a solution. I arrived at the right moment because he was about to leave for Berberati in a small plane. I was able to join him without any problem. The date and time were

People looking for diamonds around Berberati

fixed and we left. I had never seen the landscape in this way before. It usually took me a day or more and this time it only took 2 hours to cover the distance. From above we could see all the diamond and gold mines, open pit mines. It was as if the green carpet of the bush was pierced by large brown spots that indicated the places where the precious minerals were being sought. I was amazed to see so many of them. Once we arrived in Berberati, we set the time to return and I am to this day very grateful to this Minister for having transported me so generously. From the airstrip, with the help of another person present (the operator of the business from which I was buying the building materials for the chapel) at the so-called airport, I was able to drive to the exact place where I had to go. Of course, I was not able to take all my bush gear for these few days. Fortunately, there was a small hotel near the site of our new church. It was far from being comparable to what we mean by the word in Europe. But it had a bed of sorts, a kerosene lamp and some running water. Neither mosquitoes nor cockroaches were generously missing. But I was so tired at the end of the day, I fell asleep without any problem. The next day was the

31. Berberati

Sabbath. All the members, close to us and even from farther away, came to attend the feast, not to mention the local authorities. A big feast after the morning service and another evangelistic meeting later in the day ended these unforgettable moments. God was praised all day long because now He had a suitable home. Thank you Lord that by your grace we were able to complete and consecrate this place of worship. The next day, I was able to return to Bangui by the same air route, accompanied by the minister.

During one of my visits to Berberati, a church member who was a teacher in a state school came to me with a peculiar request. He had not received a salary for months. This was not surprising in a country where money is constantly in short supply. But when it is delayed for months, life becomes really hard. And he asked me if I, when I would be back in the capital, could not go to the salary offices to ask for the late payment, entrusting me with his money. He wrote a kind of power of attorney and entrusted it to me. Totally doubtful about receiving his salary, I left him assuring him that I would do my best.

When I returned a few days later, I went to the Office of Finance (teachers' salaries). Having identified myself and explained the case, I saw the official disappear into another office. To my astonishment, he then quite quickly reappeared. Looking at me and asking for my ID with a big smile, he gave me a document and accompanied me to the cashier's desk where a long line of people had already formed, probably all wanting the same thing. The employee took me in front of all the people waiting and made the cashier pay me the amount due, without any other formality and without waiting. Expressing my thanks on behalf of the person who had commissioned me, I left the payment building with great satisfaction.

A few weeks later I had to go to Berberati again for some reason. I would take the opportunity to bring the six months' salary to our brother. This time, three other brothers accompanied me by car. Shortly after leaving Bangui, a police patrol stopped us. I thought it was nothing special, just a routine check. Often after such a stop, when I said, "I am the pastor of the Adventist mission," the way was clear, but it seemed to me that this time it was different. The officer carefully examined my papers where he could not find any lack or irregularity to try to take advantage of. He circled the car and glancing inside, he noted that I had not fastened my seatbelt. Although I had never seen anyone wearing a seatbelt, he slipped it between his fingers and said to his colleagues, in the Sango language: "This one will pay, he is not my pastor." I received a ticket for riding without a seatbelt. The police officer actually wrote a ticket that would register me in the computer as a lawbreaker for riding without a seatbelt. After that, we continued on our way. We stopped to eat something a couple of hundred kilometers further on, at a place where there was a kind of stop for truckers, and I took the opportunity to check the papers that the official had given me back at the exit of the capital. I noticed that I was missing the technical control certificate. I thought that he had kept it in order to cause me problems during a possible other control a little further. This could cause me great problems in case the police stopped me without being understanding. But everything went on without further incident. We finally arrived in Berberati. In the evening, around a small fire, I told the event of the day to my colleague there. "Oh!" he said "we can go tomorrow to the gendarmerie here and explain your case to them. We are highly thought of by the chief of the station. He knows us well. He can surely do something for you." So we went to visit him the next day. We were cordially received and I was able to tell him the details of what had happened to us with complete confidence. He was very understanding and looked for a way to get us out of this ambush. After a short reflection, he came up with the following solution: "Here, Pastor, I am fining you again because you have taken a one-way street here (this does not even exist in Berberati). Because of this, instead of penalizing you financially, I have supposedly withdrawn your roadworthiness certificate for 20 days, which will do the trick." This was a clever solution that I would call a "special African solution"! Everyone was happy, especially the schoolteacher whose six months' salary I had been able to recover. After a few days spent there, mainly taking care of other business, I returned home without any of the usual problems or stops. The next Sabbath at the church in Bangui, I saw Brother Youssouf, the police commissioner, the one whose story I told above. "Don't worry", he told me, "go and see the public prosecutor and tell him what happened to you." Following our brother's advice, the following Monday I went to the public prosecutor's office, who received me without delay and did not seem in the least surprised by what I told him. " This is just more road hassle. My wife suffers from it regularly too. Don't worry, Pastor, I'll get that ticket off the computer again today." The only thing I had to do was to go through the (rather expensive) "car inspection" again to get another certificate.

32. The Restaurant

Adelheid accompanied me from time to time to this remote place. On one of these occasions, after the long journey on the dusty, tiring, and long-distance tracks, the regular checks by the police stations were, of course, part of it. So, after one of those days spent driving endlessly, we decided, after our arrival, to look for an African restaurant (there are no others) and have the evening meal. After freshening up and settling in for the night, we went looking for food. Without much effort, we found a small place that said "Restaurant." There seemed to be some good stuff on the menu. We decided to sit there. The waiter arrived soon after. We place our order with a refreshing drink. The drink was served very quickly, but the time was rather long to obtain our dish. The waiter arrived twenty minutes later but without anything to serve us. Apologizing, he tells us that our order is not available. He asks us if we would like to order something else… A bit surprised, we ordered another dish. The waiter disappeared again and he reappeared empty-handed about fifteen minutes later. He apologized again, telling us that this dish is not available either. For the third time, we looked at the menu and ordered something else in the hope that this time it will be the right one. The waiter disappeared a third time. We waited for another twenty minutes and he came back empty-handed to give us the same speech. This time, I got angry and was very surprised, but I asked him, in a very nice tone: "But my friend, tell us what there is to eat!" to which he replied, with a face full of pity for us: "Madam said there is nothing, Sir." To deal with such situations, you have to be a bit philosophical. My wife and I got up and left the restaurant. We didn't fill our stomachs that night, but we slept well because we laughed so hard, and every time we talk about it today, we still laugh. The Bible reminds us in Ecclesiastes 3:4 that there is "a time to laugh." This was one of those times!

33. Bangui and PK6 Nights

Most of the time, I/we were away as already told earlier in my story. But I have to write here how we spent the evenings when we stayed. As already mentioned before, whole evenings were spent on the stenciled machine. As they were very long, we had to find a way to occupy ourselves. Not always easy when the power is cut most of the evenings and no more water either but we still had the storm lamp, the only way to manage to read or play a family game. Before going to bed, we used to read the Bible with the help of this dim light and a spiritual book like a commentary on Paul's epistle to the Galatians or, another one whose title I remember, Revelation, with our Bible in hand, consulting verse by verse. Our reading or conversation was regularly interrupted by the army trucks that passed by at great noise and speed to control the riots that had been declared at the place known as PK6. I remember well that this was the large market located 6 kilometers from downtown. We had barricaded the doors of the house with big beams inside to avoid any surprise irruption. The situation was becoming less and less safe. Also, during our days and sometimes weeks of absence, the whole place was barricaded and a guard (named Mathias) stood guard with a bow and arrow, but we were never surprised by a robbery or anything else. We can only thank the Almighty for guarding the few possessions we had or for saving us from being subjected to physical violence. "The angel of the Lord encamps around those who fear him, and he delivers them" (Ps. 108:14, NIV)!

33. Bangui and PK6 Nights

When Adelheid had to leave and I was left alone, as mentioned above, several members of the local church visited me regularly. It was during one of these that my brother Tita told me his story.

34. PK 22

A rather strange name. But no! It was simply the place located 22 kilometers from Bangui on the road to Sibut. But each time, to get there, you had to pass several police stations and a crowd of people massing at the entrance of the city to get in or out. It was not always a pleasant experience.

Once past this grouping, the next 22 kilometers were nothing but savanna and bush on the left and right. At kilometer 22 there was a village where we had started to evangelize. A small group had formed in the

Meeting at PK22

village. Every Sabbath that we were not traveling in the country, but were on site for worship at the church in Bangui-centre or in Ngaragba (located near the famous prison), we would go to PK22 in the afternoon to visit and encourage our members. The group grew and soon we had to think about buying a piece of land to build a church. There was an old ruin of a building dating from the time of Bokassa who had planned to build a kind of factory there to operate a pineapple cannery. The place was no longer used for anything but it was exactly what we were looking for. Before I left, I was able to arrange with the surveyors of the land registry to come and fix the dimensions and place the markers. We then dug a water source, but I don't know what happened to it later.

35. The Enigma

On the road between Sibut and Bambari in the Ouaka was a developing church. We did a lot of church planting. This term entered the Adventist vocabulary of today's Europe rather late, but church planting had already been practiced for a long time in the CAR. An evangelist or even a lay member would go to a place not penetrated by our message and start preaching there. I don't remember the exact name of the place I'm talking about now, but I think it was Grimari, a fairly populated place. Every time I passed through on my way to Lower Koto or Mboumou, I stopped to visit this group and encourage them with the Word of God. It was also a good place to rest for a while after the long journey, and to refresh oneself for a moment before undertaking the last 250 dusty kilometers to the capital. For lack of a place big enough to hold people, I always preached in the open air. The former leader of the group would ask me at every opportunity, "Please pastor, give us some beams to build our chapel!" Because of a lack of funds, my answer was always the same: "Be patient, brother, we don't have any money available for beams at the moment, but it will come one day!" Weeks later, I stopped again at the same place. As I got out of the car, the brother came running up to me beaming and thanked me for the beams I had sent him. I didn't quite understand what he meant because I hadn't sent him anything. He insisted, telling me that after my last visit, a truck had come by, delivering for the Adventist Mission, exactly the number of beams they needed for the new chapel. I was stunned and have never been able to solve this riddle. Who could have delivered this shipment of wood? I guess the Lord must have sent that shipment because to my knowledge, no one ever came to claim that wood that was delivered for our church. This is how, on many occasions, we have been able to meet our God who never stops helping those who trust in Him! I think here of the text "Except the LORD builds the house, they labour in vain that build it" (Ps. 127:1).

The years passed quickly. Security in the country had become increasingly lax, so much so that it had become really dangerous to travel far from the capital. The number of highway robbers increased and they threatened travelers with handguns. We started counting the dead. On one occasion, I flew with the minister as I mentioned above. Other missions, meanwhile, lost missionaries on those roads that became dangerous. It remained a puzzle to me, why them and not us? I cannot provide an answer. The "why" and the "how" will remain questions without proper answers until the day the Lord shows us the other side of the coin.

> *This is how, on many occasions, we have been able to meet our God who never stops helping those who trust in Him!*

At some point, Adelheid had to be repatriated to Europe because of illness. I felt it was my duty to let her go and to stay behind to complete our stay. I must add that we were still waiting for the funds from ADRA to start opening the health center. The crate of equipment that we had brought with us was still stored in the garage, waiting. The only advantage of ADRA's slowness in administration was that, on many of my trips, Adelheid was able to accompany me, as I mentioned above. The remaining six months after her departure, I was mainly engaged in evangelism in Bangui and visiting members. When I left, the crate of materials we had brought for the health center was still in the garage and closed. I was never able to find out what happened to it afterwards. Two days before I left, I received a check from ADRA to start the health project. With a sad heart, I just had to return it to the sender. Thus ended our stay in Africa.

36. The Return and After…

For some time now, I have begun to consider our past life. I have turned seventy-five and I don't know how many years we have left. And now, in the autumn of my life, it is just as I read in Psalm 77:6,7: "I think of the former days, of the former years… and my spirit meditates…" Too often we live looking forward, even though we must, but let's not forget to look back as well, to count God's blessings and to meditate on how God has guided and preserved us in times of difficult choices. The many occasions when He has preserved us from misfortune or other trials in life are often quickly forgotten. The worst thing that can happen in these countries is to have a traffic accident. Thank you Lord because that has never happened to me. Everything probably didn't turn out the way we wanted or hoped, but the Lord knows why, and that's enough for me. There are ups and downs in life. Incomprehensible situations sometimes arise where we ask the question, "How and why does the Lord not intervene and why does he let it happen?" I have also experienced them. It has happened as much in our churches in Africa as in those we have here in Europe. There are not always miracles in missions, but there are also disappointments and failures, probably also because of bad decisions on our part, discouragements, ups and downs in situations that seem hopeless. I once heard a young pastor tell a typical experience that helped me a lot to solve this problem. I share it here in a few words. Traveling on a small plane, he wanted to start writing and to that end, he tried to get the small tablet out of the seat. But in this small plane, the shelves are not, as is normally the case, fixed in the chairs, but inside the sides of the plane. Pulling on his tray table, he could not get it out. After several unsuccessful attempts, other people came to his aid, but their intervention did not bring the expected result either. A flight attendant finally came and it was then that he noticed that it was noted above the window of his chair: "This is not a shelf but an emergency exit." Imagine the situation if the emergency exit had opened! Fortunately, this was not the case. Doesn't God act in the same way towards us? By not responding to all our needs, he is probably protecting us from more serious things that could happen to us. If God opened every door we asked him to open, answered every prayer we asked him to answer, we might never reach our final destination! We experience frustrations, but God probably didn't always open all the doors to keep bigger ones open! Let's keep trusting in this God who only wants our good!

Lastly, I would like to share with you a Bible text that is probably my favorite. There are many encouraging passages in the Bible, not to say that the Bible is full of them, but one of them is specific to me. It is found in Psalm 115:12: "The Lord remembers us, he will bless." Luther translates this a little differently. He says "Gott denkt an uns und segnet uns / God remembers us and blesses us." For Luther, God thinks about us all the time and blessing is not in the future but His blessing is like a daily experience.

We do not notice His blessings every moment. It is up to us to open our eyes and see! So I went back to the mainland in the course of 1992. As I mentioned above, this early return was because of the illness of my dear wife. I was reassigned to the Grand Duchy of Luxembourg to continue the evangelization work that Gerard Friedlin had been doing while we were away. (As for my wife, fortunately and by the grace of God, it was nothing serious and she soon found a new job in a local hospital). Two events especially marked me during the years that followed.

The first was the case of one of our member families. This family was confronted by the school board where they lived. Usually, to help our members obtain an exemption for their children to attend school on the Sabbath, a letter from the pastor was sufficient. This time, the teacher in charge did not accept what was usually done. From the school board, the case went to the mayor who, in turn, did not want to grant the exemption, basing himself on a text of the school law. It is worth recalling here that we had, a few years earlier, on November 26, 1982, to be precise, received a ministerial letter granting this exemption. But nothing could be done, as the mayor firmly maintained his position. When we reached this point, we asked for assistance from the conference, which intervened by sending us the head of the Religious Liberties department. But this intervention did not change anything either. The school law was still the basis. The parents were, in the meantime, threatened that the police would intervene to get the children if they did not send them to school on Saturday morning. You can imagine the state of mind of the parents. From that moment on, the case was referred to the courts. A lawyer was made available to us by the conference, which had now taken matters into its own hands. The lawyer succeeded in suspending the police intervention until a final judgment could be made. Meanwhile, the parents were also summoned to court. Under great stress and regardless of the questions asked by the magistrate, they remained firm, defending their cause. As I watched this session, I thought of the four young Israelites at Nebuchadnezzar's court in Babylon. In the end, the verdict was delivered just as the school vacations began. But what a disappointment! No consideration of religious freedom in the judgment! In a few words, the judgment said: religious freedom yes, but if it disturbs public order, it is a no. I copy here a part of the exact text which was transmitted to the parents and to our lawyer on 17/02/1998: *"...Saturday is in this case liable to disproportionately disrupt the school programs both from the point of view of the beneficiary of the derogatory scheme and of the heads of classes...* "An article appeared the next day in the Luxembourg press under the title "Administrative Court: The school obligation prevails over religion!"

What to do now? It seemed that our prayers had been in vain: all that work and stress for nothing? Yet, for months, a demand from the population was already in the air to change the weekend school order. A few weeks later, a law was voted to give the communes the autonomy to decide to adapt the school law to the population's demand. A large number of Luxembourg's communes voted for this change. Did the Lord provide an escape route? The problem has been solved once and for all for most Adventist children. This change in the law came at the right time. However, some municipalities did not adopt this change and the problem still exists to this day. In fact, a few years later (in 2000), another family in our community faced the same problem. They lived in a municipality that had not accepted the change. On March 14, 2000, one could again read in the Luxembourg press and I quote: *"Mrs. X, Minister of National Education, recently presented proposals concerning the introduction of new timetables in elementary school as of the beginning of the next school year: they mainly concern the Saturday morning lesson which, according to the formula adopted by the local authorities, could simply disappear."* However, a third family still finds itself in a difficult situation. They live in a commune that has not yet adopted the new system. They have been forced to send their child to another commune for schooling or to school at home. The latter possibility is not available to everyone. Final conclusion: Religious freedom yes, but that it does not disturb public order. All this despite a resolution that was taken by the *Parliamentary Assembly of the Council of Europe...a Resolution as well as a Recommendation...on the protection of the rights of parents and children belonging to religious minorities ... The text of the resolution has the merit to invite States to affirm and protect the right of all not to be compelled to perform actions that go against their deeply held moral or religious beliefs. (European Council for Law and Justice (ECLJ) April 2017. See full text at the end). It seems to me that this resolution has not been taken into consideration or is unknown.*

Another interesting point: In the former GDR, the school law was also primarily used to deny freedom to our children. We were bound by the law, but our brother Reinhold Paul in his book *Gott war immer der Nähe* points out that this law had nothing to do with the presence of the child for six consecutive days at school, but was rather interested in the success of the student at the end of the school year. When this goal was achieved, had the school law not been satisfied? Even when the authorities disagreed, the children did not attend school on the Sabbath and the teachers were instructed to report to their superiors only those cases where the children were deficient or did not do well enough. This was never the case, so the chapter was closed. It should also be noted that in this atheist and 150% communist country, the school law could be circumvented more easily than in our democracies which congratulate themselves on their "religious freedom" and sing it from the rooftops. Freedom of conscience was more respected in the communist countries than here!

In 1996, Hans Obenaus contacted me to ask if I would be available to go to Senegal. He was serving with his wife Sylvie at our station in Casamance. Sylvie was in charge of the dispensary attached to the mission station. They were soon to go to Mauritania to begin ADRA's work in this new territory. It turned out that Adelheid and I were the ideal couple to replace them there. But before passing our names on to the division, he wanted to know what I thought. It was difficult to answer so quickly. I was reluctant because evangelization was in full swing in the Grand Duchy. Also, I would have liked to see the place before we started. My wife advised me to go and see it before we decided. So I asked for a 10-day leave to go there. So I went to Senegal. To go from Dakar (the capital) to Casamance, you have to cross the whole south of the country. Daniel Cordas, who was the president of the mission in Senegal at that time, was not there. Hans showed me the main part of the mission, taking me also to Guinea Bissau where he had to go to cash a check from ADRA. For a few thousand US dollars, we had to carry bags full of local bills. I don't remember exactly how much or how much they weighed, but they were certainly heavy. At the end of this visit and after about ten days, we prayed for God's grace, for the Lord to guide us in our decision. Finally we did not accept it and later on, this decision proved to be wise. Thank you Lord!

36. The Return and After... **147**

The next case took place in 1997. Since our definitive return to our homeland, I had mostly been involved in conferences and Five Day Plans. Also, at the International Fair of Luxembourg (FIL), we had a stand to make our health work known through our Five Day Plans. One day, I received a request from Hans Obenaus, who was then in charge of ADRA in Mauritania, who suggested that I go to Nouakchott to help him start the implementation of Five Day Plans in Mauritania.

He had asked the UFB for help but the answer was clear: Mauritania was not part of their territory. So he called on me. I then contacted our BL Conference president who, I think, probably had a broader view of our church and gave me permission to go there without any problem. After contacting our division in Bern again, the costs of the trip were taken care of by the division, out of the ADRA department's expenses. A few weeks later I flew back to Africa. Upon my arrival in Nouakchott, we visited several officials and a few days later we met in a large hall provided by the city to inaugurate the first Five Day Plan in this large Muslim country. A large

Five Day Plans stand at the International Fair of Luxembourg

number of people were present. We even had the presence of the Mauritanian television and radio one evening . They did most of the publicity. I was not too surprised to find myself the next evening on the television screens of the country. Once back at my GD workplace, I continued to evangelize in a country so closed to the Gospel. Here is another episode to explain the difficulties encountered. I was informed of this as soon as I arrived by one of the members present in the country.

Shortly before Brother F. Lecompte started here, one of his children had decided to go to Luxembourg to peddle to earn the money necessary to pay his school fees. He was quickly arrested by the police because in the GD door-to-door sales are forbidden. The poor young man was taken to the police station and questioned. If I remember correctly, as I was told, his father had to come and get him out of this uncomfortable situation. At the end of the story, since the Belgian was not aware of the law prohibiting peddling, he was allowed to return, but his books were confiscated. After my return from Mauritania, I continued to go door-to-door, not to sell books, but with an "opinion poll" about certain points of the Christian faith, in order to find potential interested parties. It seems to me, however, that one day someone must have observed me behind curtains while I was walking from one house to another and that this person must have alerted the police because a mobile patrol arrived a few minutes later, arrested me and questioned me because door-to-door sales work was not yet allowed. After I declared my identity and explained my occupation of the moment, they gave me back my freedom but I did not let them go without asking them the questions of my "opinion poll" which they kindly wanted to answer. Since then, the law has changed and door-to-door work is now authorized.

I must interject here an episode that showed me how ignorant people are about religion and faith, but which personally taught me a strong lesson about the grace of God. That evening I had to go to an address that was a bit problematic and I was asking myself the question, "How do I solve the problem?" The address was far away and it was already dark. Lost in my thoughts, I hadn't noticed that at one point the speed limit was 60 and I was doing 70. A little further on, there was a mobile patrol to stop those in a hurry. I was now guilty of breaking the law. After a nice greeting, the policeman pointed out that my speed was not in accordance with the prescribed speed. This would cost me quite a bit since the rates had increased again the week before. What to say in such a situation? After asking for my papers, the policeman asked me what I did for a living. "I'm a pastor," I said, to which the officer of the law retorted, "What's that?" "Preacher of grace," I said and I added, "Behold, now the preacher of grace has fallen under the condemnation of the law." But the man doesn't seem to understand anything and continues to ask me, "What is a preacher?" "A preacher is a Protestant minister, as a priest is an officiant in the Catholic church." But this answer seemed to confuse the good officer more and more. "I don't understand. Explain it to me again," he said. And I repeated: "The pastor, the preacher of grace, has fallen under the condemnation of the law." But this repetition does not seem to have enlightened or convinced him. Probably reaching the end of his Latin, he says to me, "Here are your papers and be careful in the future!" I had to smile a little after that incident, but that evening never went out of my head and gave me time to think. Isn't it the same for each of us when faced with our guilt and divine forgiveness? I was guilty of a transgression that would cost me dearly! But I received a pardon that saved me from a heavy fine. Since that night, I always pay double attention to the speed limit. There is always a reason to stick to the rules because they want to avoid accidents. Do I do the same with the divine advice concerning my way of life? The truth is that I do what I want, but God wants the best for me. So I do well to pay attention to His advice because He wants to protect me from disaster. This does not only apply overseas but wherever we are sent. That is why I have also told some episodes of my work in Europe.

Missionary work has always been a passion for me and the former missionaries have always set an example for us (my wife and I). Yet, how much can we compare to them? As I read *A Daughter Remembers* written by Lydie, the daughter of D.E. Delhove, the first Belgian missionary who left in 1913, it became clear to me what these people sacrificed and left behind. Today we fly to Africa and arrive at our destination in one or two days. This was not the case in those days. Lydie Delhove describes in her book how it took five long months from Europe to get to the shores of Lake Rwanda by boat, train, then again by boat, long walks through the bush, by dugout canoe, etc. She writes: *"We had traveled from the north to the south of the country by boat and then by train."* She writes: *"We had traveled 2,400 miles across Africa from the Atlantic Ocean. Five long months had passed since we left Europe... It was August 1919."* (Delhove, Lydie. *A Daughter Remembers D. E. Delhove: Pioneer Missionary in Central Africa*. Self-published, 1984). Once at their destination, they had to start building (temporary) houses, preach the gospel, and when they got sick, apart from some native treatments, the only thing they could do was pray to God for intervention. Communications were long in those days, it often took months for a letter to arrive from Europe. Because of this, our pioneers regularly had to rely on their own judgment in emergency situations. In a letter from David Delhove dated July 11, 1942, he wrote to his daughter Lydia, "On our knees we placed ourselves in the hands of God who never failed to answer our pleas." David passed away in January 1949, but he was a pioneer of Adventist work in Africa and what a testimony he left! After his burial on African soil, a man came to Lydia and said, "You know, your father was a true Christian. I did not share the same beliefs but I had a lot of admiration for him. He not only had faith in his religion but he lived it." A testimony that makes me think again. Can the same be said of me?

In the previous pages, I have written what I thought essential to transmit as a testimony of our experience with God. The time of the missionaries coming from Europe or the USA is partly over nowadays. But fortunately, the work that was started in these countries, often under the most difficult circumstances, continues. We were a bit like the third and last missionary generation and we thank God for what we were able to accomplish during that time. This work, initiated by the Lord, continues today and it is regrettable that so many churches have abandoned the missionary report that allows us to see how the Adventist work often progresses in difficult, not to say dangerous, situations. There are still brothers and sisters in our church today who leave their homeland to serve in an overseas country, perhaps not so much in Africa anymore but in other parts of the world, especially in Asia.

We cannot become self-centered churches. This is also partly necessary because we need our local churches to grow as well. But we cannot forget that we are part of a worldwide movement and that "the field is the world" (Matt. 13:38). The end of the story: Each of us is a missionary in the field around us and each of us could have our own experiences. It is enough to open our eyes daily to see the miracles of God and to have experiences with Him.

In closing, a final word for reflection. A rabbi once asked his students, "Where is God?" After a time of reflection, one after another began to answer. "In heaven," said one student. "In nature," said another. "In the library," said a third. "In the synagogue," said a fourth. Each time, the rabbi's answer was "no." The students were getting impatient and were now asking the rabbi to give the answer because they did not understand. Finally, all relaxed and confident, the rabbi said, "God is wherever you invite him." What a great truth! Yes, God is where we invite him. Don't forget to invite him every day! But how can I feel the presence of the Lord? This is a good question and I have heard it often. People have asked me many times. I always have the same answer. It is found in Psalm 139:5: "You surround me from behind and from before and put your hand on me." This gives me confidence. He surrounds me! I probably don't always feel it, but the fact that He is near me remains. "God surrounds us" and we need to experience this every day! God never leaves us alone. When we leave Him out that's when we are alone, but we don't want that truth. We feel too deprived of our freedom and we prefer to live without God. There is no need to describe here

> *Each of us is a missionary in the field around us and each of us could have our own experiences. It is enough to open our eyes daily to see the miracles of God and to have experiences with Him.*

what we reap when we live without him: murder, suicide, drugs with all their harmful consequences, crime, and you can make the list longer.

Again, at the end of World War II, at the Nuremberg Trials (1945-46), Hans Frank, who was the Governor General of Poland for the NAZI regime, known as the "Butcher of Poland," had, it seems to me, a clear vision of things. He said at the end of his plea, "It seems to me that at the beginning of our path we could not have thought that our setting aside of God could produce such evil, murderous, and execrable consequences... Thus, by our neglect of God, we have become a disgrace and should disappear." When we neglect God, the end is always tragic!

Now, so many years later, my heart is still somewhat attached to Africa, a land I love and to which I return on certain occasions. I have left many friends there. What a joy it was for me to meet several of them or their descendants at the General Conference in San Antonio in 2015! It was moving to meet the next generation. The work, once begun, is continued by a generation full of strength and the love of Christ. Today, twenty years later, our Europe is overwhelmed by African brothers and sisters who, for one reason or another, had to leave their native countries. They are the ones who have become our missionaries here in our countries, and we can say how fortunate we are because they are the ones who fill our churches these days and Adventism can continue to exist. In Matthew 27:32, we read that a certain man, Simon of Cyrene, was forced to carry the cross of Jesus. Note here that Cyrene was a large city in North Africa. Should Adventists from Africa now carry the Adventist message into our modern Europe? It seems to me. Has Europe become a culture that no longer needs Jesus?

Let me end with what I just read somewhere and I think it is a thought of Saint-Exupery and still valid today:

"When people start living without God,

Governments are perplexed

People without peace

Endless debts

Conversations without results

Brainless enlightenment
Politicians without character
Christians without prayer
Churches without strength
Lies without end
The unbridled morals
Fashion without shame
Endless crime
Endless congress
Desolate perspectives"
Is the world of modern culture like this?

"God has given me two sons, one for me and one for God."

Let it be so. This remark (from my father to his mother), so quick and convincing, has followed me to this day.

"The Lord shall preserve thy going out and thy coming in from this time forth, and even for evermore" (Ps. 121:8).

What better way than to give testimony of how God, the Lord Jesus Christ, has led me through the experiences I have had with Him. May His name be praised, and may these instances that have permeated my memory and my life serve as an inspiration for others to trust in the One who never leaves us without His presence.

Marc D. Cools

TEACH Services, Inc.
PUBLISHING

We invite you to view the complete
selection of titles we publish at:
www.TEACHServices.com

We encourage you to write us
with your thoughts about this,
or any other book we publish at:
info@TEACHServices.com

TEACH Services' titles may be purchased in
bulk quantities for educational, fund-raising,
business, or promotional use.
bulksales@TEACHServices.com

Finally, if you are interested in seeing
your own book in print, please contact us at:
publishing@TEACHServices.com

We are happy to review your manuscript at no charge.